JEWELS
IN THE LOUVRE

PUBLICATIONS

Musée du Louvre

Violaine Bouvet-Lanselle
Director of Cultural Development
Head of Publications

Fanny Meurisse
Editorial Coordination and Photo Research

Flammarion

Sophy Thompson
Director, Illustrated Books

Translated from the French
by David Radzinowicz
Design: Isabelle Ducat
Copyediting: Lindsay Porter
Typesetting: Gravemaker+Scott
Proofreading: Anne Korkeakivi
Color Separation: Reproscan, Italy
Printed in Malaysia by Tien Wah Press

AUTHORS

Adrien Goetz, prominent French art historian, is editor-in-chief of *Grande Galerie* and *Le Journal du Louvre*. He has published numerous books on subjects such as Ingres' collages and the collections of French museums. He has also written award-winning fiction, always with art as a central theme. In 2007 he was decorated with a prestigious award from the Academy Française (le grand prix François-Victor Noury of the Institut de France).

Claudette Joannis is a head curator at the national museum of Malmaison in France, where she is responsible for textiles and jewelry. She has curated several exhibitions on jewels, and has written exhibition catalogues and contributed to an international dictionary of jewelry.

Editor's Note: All measurements of the works are given in height by width unless otherwise indicated.

Distributed in North America by Rizzoli International Publications, Inc.

Simultaneously published in French as *Bijoux*

08 09 10 3 2 1

Dépôt legal: 10/2008

Louvre ISBN: 978-2-35031-194-4
Flammarion ISBN: 978-2-0803-0078-2

www.louvre.fr
www.editions.flammarion.com

JEWELS
IN THE LOUVRE

ADRIEN GOETZ
CLAUDETTE JOANNIS

MUSÉE DU LOUVRE ÉDITIONS
Flammarion

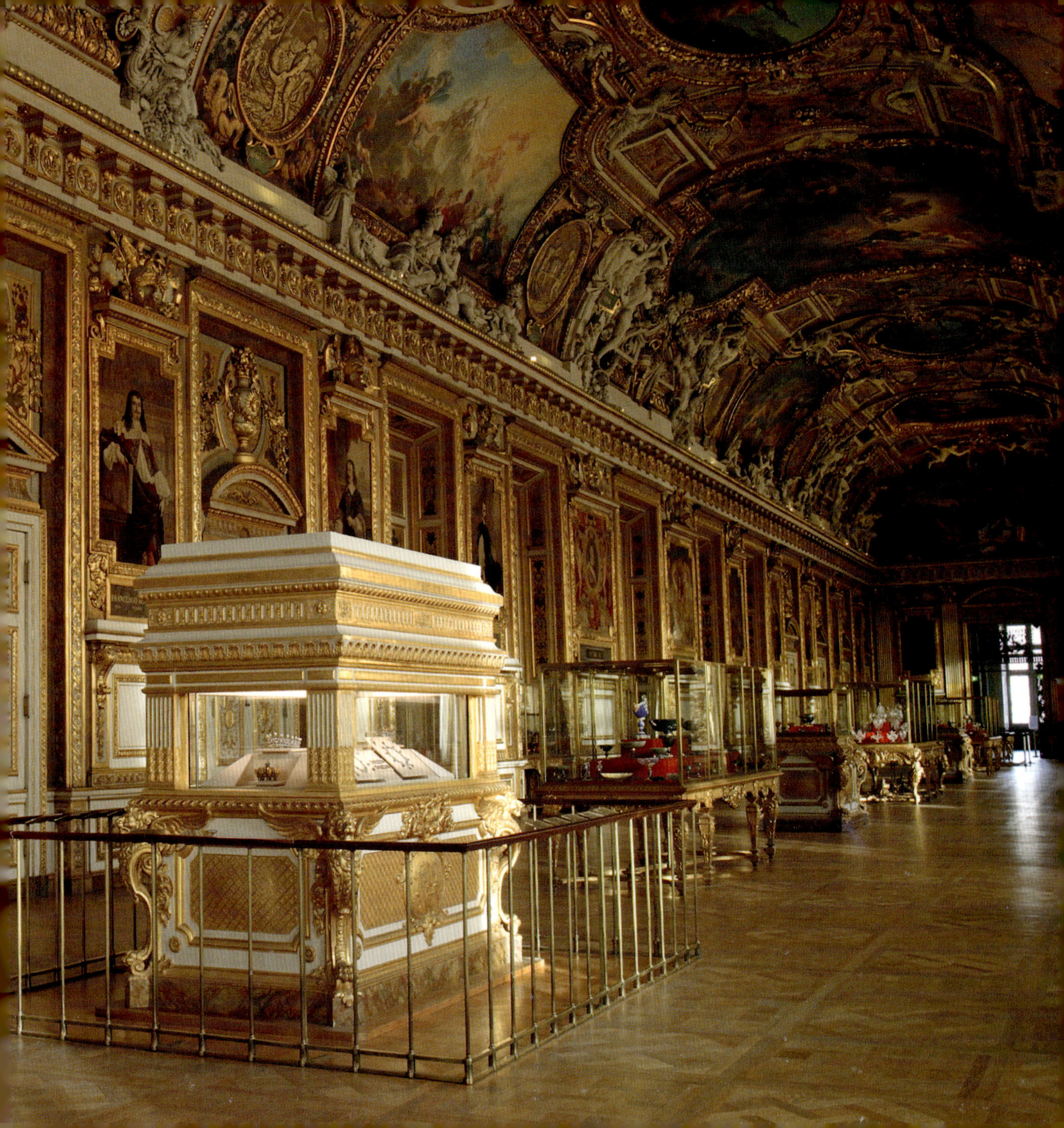

PREFACE
by **Adrien Goetz**

All things considered [...] if a woman's adventures *must* be divulged, better it be by her jewels than by her lover.

Denis Diderot, *The Indiscreet Jewels*

"But the long-lost jewels of antique Palmyra,/Metals unknown, pearls of the sea..." Was Baudelaire thinking of a museum when he wrote the most beautiful lines in his poem "Bénédiction"? The treasures of Palmyra are not in the Louvre. Nor are they in the sands of Syria. Exactly what gems archaeologists might uncover among the ruins of the capital of the legendary Queen Zenobia mattered little to the author of *Les Fleurs du mal*. Because these long-lost jewels, these *bijoux perdus*, are pure poetry, enamels and cameos that Baudelaire borrows, so as to "transform" them, from his master Théophile Gautier's *Émaux et Camées*. In 1857, readers of *Les Fleurs du Mal* would read a few pages further on how "Many a jewel lies interred/In darkness and oblivion,/Far from the pick-axes and probes." Their beauty resides in invisibility. The writer—the seer—assures readers that such jewels do exist somewhere, beneath the sand, under the sea, within the stuff of the text. The poet sees himself as an archaeologist; his pen does the excavating, his book is the museum. As if in confirmation, in 1861 France acquired the jewels of the Campana Collection, comprising Greek, Etruscan, and Roman treasures. They were unveiled to the public, first at the Palais de l'Industrie the following year and then in the Louvre where they remain, a source of wonder to all who visit them and an enduring source of inspiration to craftsmen.

The Apollo Gallery
Paris, Musée du Louvre

Paradoxically, showing visitors jewels from the remote past—in showcases and not on flesh or sewn to rich fabrics or locked up in jewel cases—is a way of opening—not closing—the doors of the imagination. Does a pearl necklace perish because no one wears it? No, it doesn't, as the Louvre proves. Empress Eugénie's pearl-and-diamond diadem is doing fine. A jewel, unearthed by a digger's spade, snatched from the treasury of a prince by revolutionaries, or off the scales of a money-changer and put in the Louvre beguiles us because one can sense within it both the romantic spirit and the yawning chasm of time.

The expression "historic jewel" must be taken in its fullest extension. The Côte de Bretagne, a spinel of more than 100 carats since cut into a little dragon for Louis XV, has come down to us intact behind armor-plated glass, inalienable State property since Francis I. Other fragile regal masterpieces also managed to survive the vagaries of fashion, the ransacking of the Royal Garde-Meuble—or the Royal Depository—in September 1792, and the disastrous sale of the Crown diamonds by the Third Republic in 1887. Cardinal Richelieu's carriage watch escaped the grasping fingers of the privy purse. A small gold niello ring, a seventh-century Byzantine memento of a wedding of which nothing further is known, miraculously endured the storms of history before being presented to the Louvre by the Marquis de Boisgelin in 1968. For every piece tells a story: that's what fortunate owners of "prestige" treasures need to be convinced of. They need to learn the names of Rothschild, of Fould-Springer, Sauvageot, Davillier, Révoil, Lenoir, Schlichting, Heine, Olivier, and Côte, all generous donors of jewels, snuffboxes, or timepieces, and see all the noble yet anonymous gifts and the treasures acquired by the Amis du Louvre.

The observation might make one squirm, but it's a fact: for its owner's family, a jewel remains forever an accessory of the drama of bourgeois life. Think of Maupassant's *La Parure* or the earrings in Louise de Vilmorin's novel, *Madame de*, or the Eustace diamonds of Anthony Trollope's novel. In her moving memoirs, Isabelle, Comtesse de Paris, and the last woman to wear the diamond and sapphire ornament that had been the pride and joy of Queen Hortense and Queen Marie-Amélie, recounts how she gave it a codename: "my chocolates." Isn't it an improvement to see these "chocolates" liberated from their ridiculous vaudeville casket and on show instead in the Gallery of Apollo? Owners of legendary gems, think of the Louvre! Turn your backs on the bank vault and the silver paper. For a jewel in a museum becomes a talisman. Sloughing off mere vanity and fame, it is charged with history and mystery. It becomes beyond price. Hence the profound poetry, intuited by Baudelaire, that a diamond straight out of the cutter's workshop and placed in some shop window in Paris's Place Vendôme can never possess and which, in a world where the art of the conversation is in its death throes, it seems to have lost even in candlelight.

Today the public entering the museum by the glass Pyramid—that diamond as big as the Louvre—comes to gawp at the "Treasury of France." Tourists might well be disappointed for France does not have its Tower of London, Edinburgh Castle, Budapest Parliament, Kremlin, Hradcany, or even its treasure chamber in the Castle of Kropow (that last one's from Tintin's *King Ottokar's Sceptre*), and the jewels of monarchical ritual have for the majority been lost or dispersed. Instead, the great showcases in the Gallery of Apollo parade, in full view, the monogram RF, the seal of the French Republic, a forthright political statement that dates from its third incarnation. Such a choice of display possesses a deep meaning and should be pondered. Elsewhere in the museum, in the medieval rooms of the Department of Decorative Arts, certain pieces of regalia seem quite at home. Others are at Reims, in the Palais du Tau, together with the Talisman of Charlemagne, presented at the close of World War I by an Empress Eugénie still draped in widow's weeds. Pointedly, she did not bequeath it to the Louvre, and the museum does not house her "treasure."

The Gallery of Apollo presents under one roof the bracelets of the Duchesse d'Angoulême, a court parure; the personal crown of Louis XV, a political ornament; and the gleaming Star of the Order of the Holy Spirit—insignia or jewel, it is hard to say. The Regent diamond was stuck on a hat to hold Louis XV's aigrette in place. It is as if, for the Louvre, any jewel might have been used to crown emperor or king. As if the least historical carbuncle is liable to become a jewel of the motherland.

The point is less that the Regent weighs more than 140 carats: many a paperweight can beat that—especially since the British had the crafty idea of plundering the mines of the Transvaal. What is interesting is that it was mounted on Napoleon Bonaparte's sword when he was first consul. What makes one stop to think is that it owes its name to one of France's greatest writers, Saint-Simon, who recounts, with some latitude, how he managed to hoodwink the French Regent, Philippe d'Orléans, into purchasing it. It's the "carats" of history and literature that weigh most. What counts is the Sancy Blood Diamond, the Affair of the Queen's Necklace—though not the one the ill-fated Marie-Antoinette was never to see, but the one the gentleman thief Arsène Lupin lifted, in his first adventure by Maurice Leblanc. In a movie of 1937, *Les Perles de la Couronne*, Sacha Guitry shot the mind-boggling story of a historic jewel in a succession of set-piece *tableaux*. Jewels in a museum could tell whole books of such stories.

Is this just history with a small "h"—merely anecdote and tittle-tattle? That is already good enough. The Sancy, the Hortensia, the Mazarins, the Côte de Bretagne are all legends. The jewels in the Louvre—Egyptian pendants, Assyrian seals, or amulets from Ancient Rome—have become jewels in another, far more universal crown. Anonymous or signed by master goldsmiths or jewellers, jewels from less distant times are works of art in their own right. Jewelers Nitot, Menière, Bapst, Froment-Meurice, Lemonnier, and Castellani were real artists—great ones. They are worthy of being in the Louvre, next to the Old Masters and foremost sculptors of their time.

For the jewels in the Louvre also include those which painters pinned or hung, for all eternity, on their models. Are they imaginary? La Bella Nanni in her all finery posing before Veronese—is she real? Are the guests at the Wedding at Cana wearing authentic Venetian jewels, gemstones whose "water" the artist has transmuted into paint? Certain pieces, reverently preserved today by the descendants of the sitters, are valuable specifically because they were painted by Ingres. More must surely exist somewhere and may resurface one day. Where are Monsieur Rivière's intaglios and his charms? And where are the tiny rose-cut diamonds worn by Madame Marcotte?

Such fables surrounding jewelry can raise a smile. Thank heaven, then, the museum also incites visitors to throw off their trinkets, presenting them with the example of the black-clad gentlemen of the Port Royal—the seventeenth-century philosophers, known as the *Solitaires*—who were considered the incarnation of noble simplicity, possessing a serene grandeur that transcended physical nudity. "How these vain ornaments, how these veils weigh upon me," Racine's Phèdre could aptly say, descending with you into a museum and divesting herself of her glad-rags... And although Chassériau's Esther dresses up for Assuerus, Foyatier's Spartacus stands as nature intended. His slave-chains—his *esclavage*—are made of bronze, and have nothing to do with the fashionable necklace of the same name. Throughout its checkered history, jewelry has been threatened by a recurrent tendency to sobriety: the application of the sumptuary laws in ancient Rome and under France's fourteenth-century king, Philippe le Bel, the gifts of gold made to the nation when war loomed. In France, it all started with the baptism of its first Christian king, Clovis, in the fifth century: *depende collas sicamber* (put off your necklaces), St. Remi thundered—enough to make an archaeologist blanch. Another locus classicus of this penchant for asceticism: the exemplary life of the noblest daughter of Scipio Africanus, Cornelia, mother of the Gracchi, as painted by Joseph-Benoit Suvée in a magnificent neoclassical picture conserved in the Louvre.

The scene is lifted from Plutarch but occurs in Cornelius Nepos and Valerius Maximus as well. She points to her children and cries: "These are my only jewels." She gets on our nerves though. For she forces us to think, to wonder about this primeval fascination for all that shines, for all things gold.

As a finale to his "Poème sur les pierreries", and following a cascade of quatrains entitled, in accordance with a subtle alternation of plural and singular, *Pearls*, *Emerald*, *Rubies*, *Sapphire,* and *Diamonds*, Jean Cocteau pens the following envoi:

A beautiful couple lives in the Louvre
The Mona Lisa *and the Regent*
But your eyes when you open them
Make such treasures look poor.

The woman who seems to have anticipated the poet's exhortation most completely gazes out in unimpeachable purity from a painting by Camille Corot. No one knows her name and no one can agree even when it was painted. It is a museum piece, calculated to resemble the *Mona Lisa* and a little the *Belle Ferronnière* too. Tradition has it that she was called *The Woman with the Pearl.* But no one has ever seen a pearl on her forehead. Perhaps, scrutinizing this beautiful, unadorned woman more closely, one can just distinguish above the eye line a miniscule shell threaded onto a ribbon—an adornment of no value, invented by the artist. For us today the jewels of Palmyra exist only through Baudelaire. A jewel more valuable than any other, immaterial and abstract, that nonexistent pearl in the portrait of an unknown woman is the mystery of Corot. And it is the triumph of art.

SELECTED WORKS

Text by **Claudette Joannis**

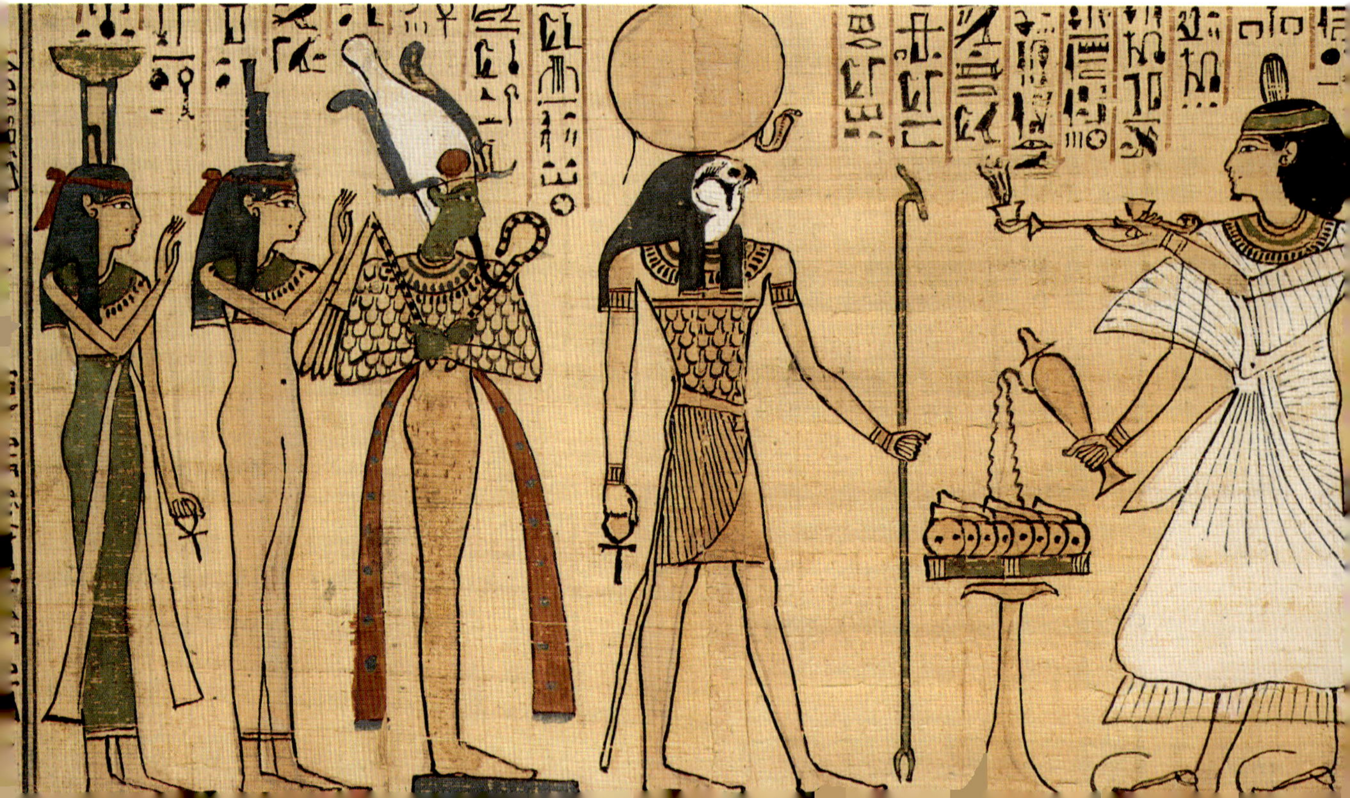

1. **ANONYMOUS** (Right)
Mummy necklace from the tomb of Chancellor Nakhti
Egypt, 1950–1900 BCE
Siliceous earthenware beads, 7 × 10 ⅝ in. (17.5 × 27 cm)

2. **ANONYMOUS**
The Book of the Dead of Khonsumes
Egypt, nineteenth dynasty, c. 1295–1186 BCE
Painted papyrus, 10 × 157 ½ in. (26 cm × 4 m)

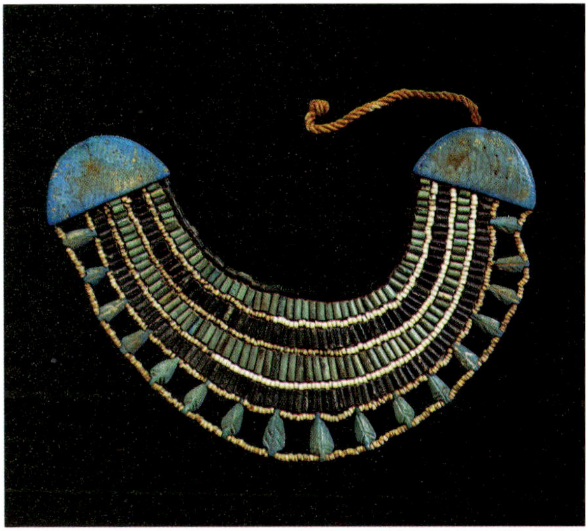

1. Figures on the funerary paintings and sculptures of Ancient Egypt often sport a wide, multi-row necklace. Worn by both men and women for nearly three thousand years, from the Old Empire to the collapse of Dynastic Egypt, this adornment, known as a *wesekh*, can be variously seen as a pectoral, gorgerin, or collarets. Although such necklaces could be presented to guests at banquets, they also entered the world of the dead and were placed among the burial goods intended to accompany the deceased on his or her final journey. This polychrome earthenware necklace, made chiefly of green tubular beads alternating with smaller white ones, was unearthed among other everyday articles in the tomb of a notable from the end of the Middle Empire, the chancellor Nakhti. The beads are combined with a row of leaf-shaped motifs, although lotus flowers were also frequent. The clasp, made of two broad semicircular earthenware discs, might take the shape of the head of the falcon Horus, a funerary emblem. It retains a fragment of string that shows the rudimentary type of fastener with which such pectorals were commonly secured.

2. The accuracy of the funerary scenes from the Pharaonic period that were painted in sarcophagi and on tomb walls can be gauged from this procession, which features the gods Osiris and Horus, women bearing offerings, and the deceased himself. All sport a broad pectoral, the making of which can be seen in other tomb paintings showing craftsmen using bow-drills to bore the beads, with others threading them, or else handing the finished product to the pharaoh.

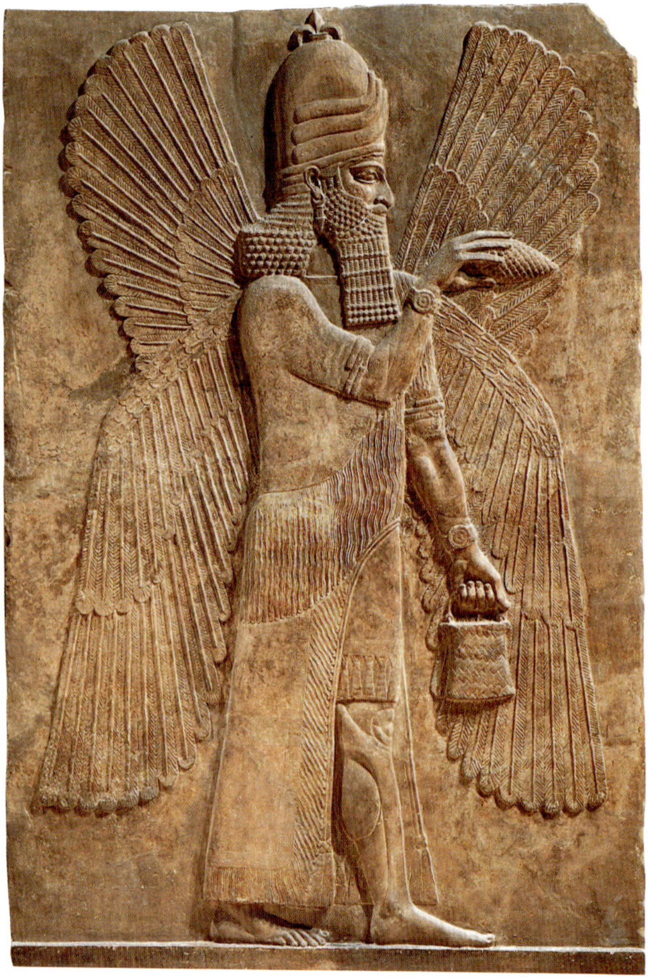

ANONYMOUS
Winged genius in the act of blessing and carrying a situla
Bas-relief from the frontage to the palace of Sargon II in Khorsabad, c. 710 BCE, reign of Sargon II
Limestone, 10 ft. 10 in. × 7 ft. ¼ in. (3.30 × 2.14 m)

An integral part of Assyrian iconography, this winged figure comes from the palace at Khorsabad and was discovered by archaeologists some time between 1852 and 1854. The edifice was lined in carved bas-reliefs recounting the noble deeds of Sargon II, the king who built a complex that was to stand in the center of a new city that was never finished.

Processions of soldiers and dignitaries run for miles along the frontages and in the courtyards of the palace. There are also priests, servants, and guardian geniuses, who sprinkle ritual water over a tree, the symbol of life. All are richly dressed in fringed tunics, while their carefully crimped beards and hair speak of their high rank. Invariably, their arms, necks, and ears are decorated with jewelry. The majestic genius here, capped with a miter and holding in one hand a bucket-like vessel (*situla*) and in the other a pine-cone, parades no less than four bracelets, two open ones on the arms and two closed ones adorned with rosettes on the wrists, as well as pendants about his ears. The wearing of gold bracelets on the wrists and above the elbows was reserved for the king and higher dignitaries. In the ancient Orient, such ornaments were regarded as symbols of royalty and nobility.

In Rome, on the other hand, a mere private soldier might receive a bracelet (*armilla*) as a reward for his valor. The plain or jointed bracelets found in Egyptian, Etruscan, as well as Iranian tombs demonstrate that this kind of ornament fulfilled both a symbolic and decorative purpose.

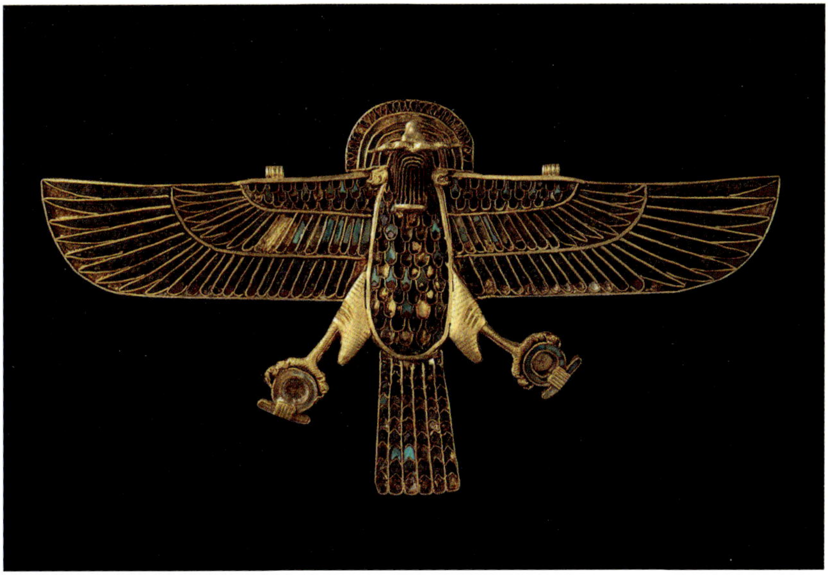

ANONYMOUS
Pectoral in the shape of a vulture with a ram's head
Egypt, reign of Ramses II, nineteenth dynasty, c. 1295–1186 BCE
Serapeum of Saqqara
Gold, carnelian, lapis lazuli, and turquoise, 2 ¾ × 5 in. (7 × 13 cm)

For the Egyptians, jewels, in daily life as well as in the world beyond, were something to be worn equally by gods, goddesses, and mere mortals. As for many other peoples in antiquity, these adornments indicated the wearer's role, but they also might serve as a talisman, a reward, or a means of payment. They were often placed on the more vulnerable points of the body, such as the temples or round the stomach or neck.

This pectoral of the image of the vulture goddess Nekhabit, represented with wings outstretched, is made of gold and fine stones, precious stones in the true sense being unknown in Egypt.

Turquoises from the Sinai are combined with carnelian, red amber, and lapis lazuli to make cloisonné necklaces and pectorals. Cloissoné consists of small partitions raised over a metal ground to form minute compartments that are then filled with colored molten glass or stones. This technique was to attain its zenith in the New Empire.

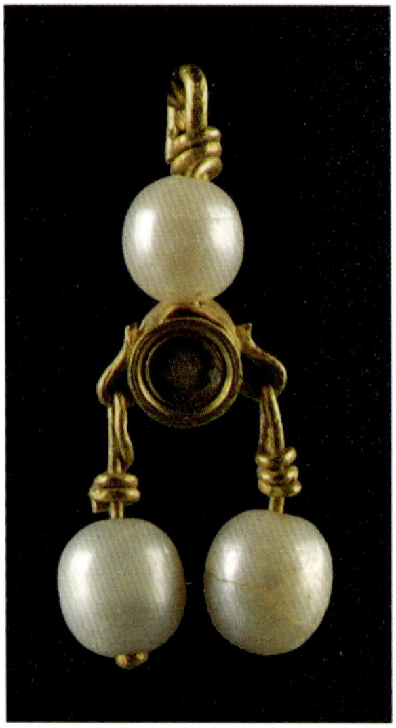

1. **ANONYMOUS** (Facing page)
Portrait of a woman
Antinoe, Roman Egypt, second century CE
Encaustic-painted wood, 14 ½ × 6 ⅝ in. (36.8 × 17 cm)

2. **ANONYMOUS**
Earrings
Roman Egypt, end of the second century–beginning of the third century CE
Gold and pearls, 1 in. (2.5 cm)

1. This portrait comes from the Roman necropolis of Antinoe, the district capital of Fayum, a region southwest of Cairo. Cartonnage bust pieces as well as these portraits painted on wood have been uncovered by archeologists at this site. In the second century CE, Egypt was under Roman rule: rich Egyptians, afraid of losing their identity in the beyond, would sit for a portrait painted on a wood panel that would then be affixed to the head of their mummy in what was a common funerary practice aimed at smoothing the passage from life to death. Among these portraits, those of the women—"Orientals with eyes like almahs," as Marcel Proust put it—are particularly touching.

This young woman has been painted in all her finery, allowing her to appear for all eternity as she did in life. With an artful hairstyle and her eyes ringed with kohl, she is bedecked in choice jewelry in a Hellenistic style: pearl earrings and a necklace made of beads in a dark emerald-green crystal separated by grains of gold. Roman women also adopted this fashion. Similar jewels have been unearthed in tombs.

2. These earrings, almost identical to those in the portrait, consist of three pearls, including two hanging on either side of a gold disc. Rare in the Pharaonic period, pearls from the Persian Gulf and then from the Red Sea became all the rage in the Roman era. Emperor Caligula (12–41 CE) presented a necklace of pearls to his horse, while Nero (37–68 CE) made his actors wear masks drenched in pearls on stage. During the same period, certain patricians brave enough to risk ripping their ears with the sheer weight of their pearls would hang several from each lobe. In his *De Beneficis* ("Of Benefits"), Seneca remarks that the value of such pearls could be equivalent to an entire estate.

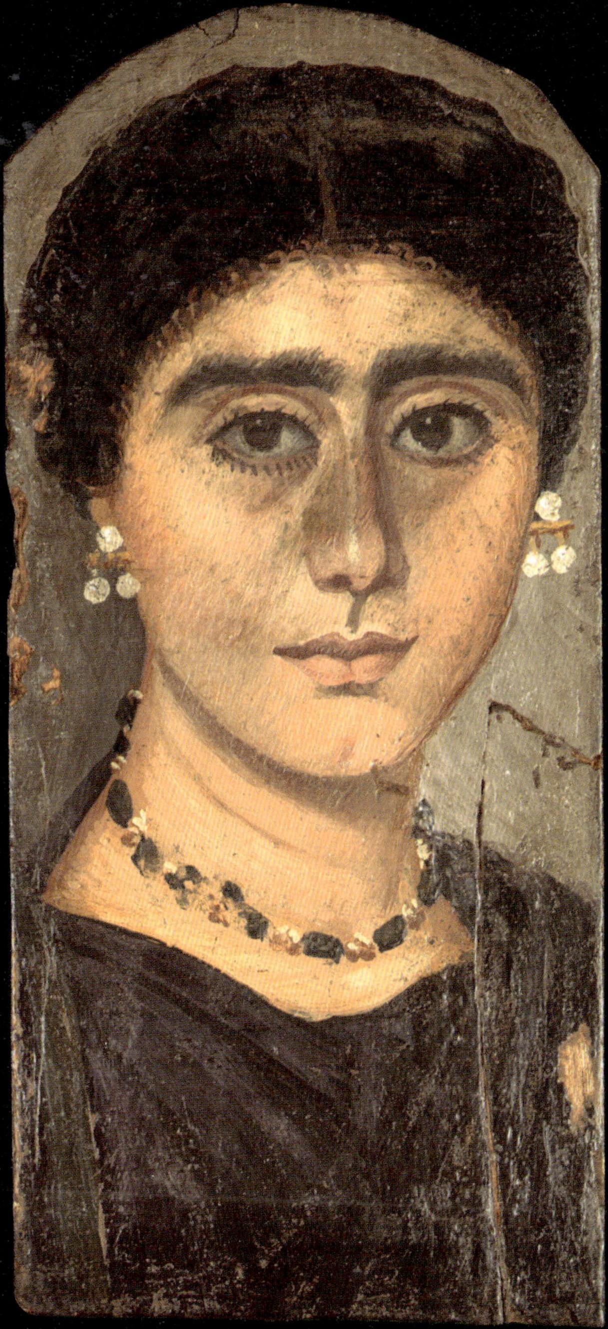

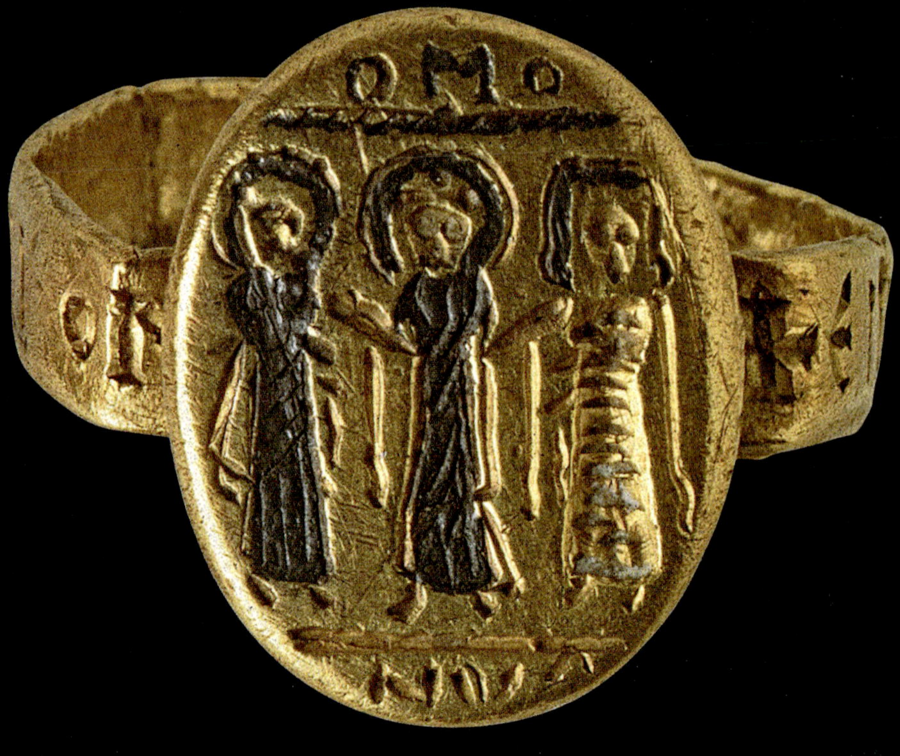

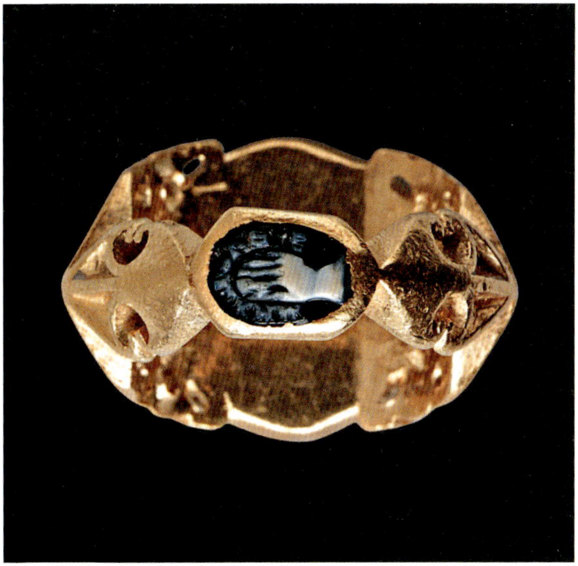

1. **ANONYMOUS**
Wedding ring
Byzantium, seventh century CE
Gold and niello, d. ¾ in. (2 cm)

2. **ANONYMOUS**
Ring with crossed hands
Roman world, third century CE
Gold and nicolo, d. 1 1⁄16 in. (2.7 cm)

Separated by several centuries, these two rings nonetheless share one and the same theme: love and faithfulness. Rings already formed part of the wedding ritual in the early Christian era, and were given by the husband-to-be to the bride as a guarantee of mutual fidelity. On the Byzantine wedding band (1), the central section of the mount, oval in shape, represents the couple standing before Christ and receiving His blessing. The scene is framed by the legend *OMONOIA*, which means "harmony." These marriage bands, in silver or in engraved and nielloed gold, have been found in Syria and Constantinople.

A pair of crossed hands was a rather longer-lived motif, and had already developed in the Roman era. At that time, it was a simple iron ring given to the future wife as a sign of her engagement and was decorated with two clasped hands and featured inscriptions. This is the case with the ring (2), on which the form of two crossed hands has been hollowed out (a process known as intaglio) of a slate-gray agate. On the reverse, a hand is shown pinching an ear, accompanied by an inscription in Greek. These rings became more widespread from the second century, when they became known as *fede* in Italy, and *bonne foi* in France. They continued to exist in Europe for centuries; in nineteenth-century Brittany, for example, such bands were called *bagues d'accordailles*—"troth-plight rings".

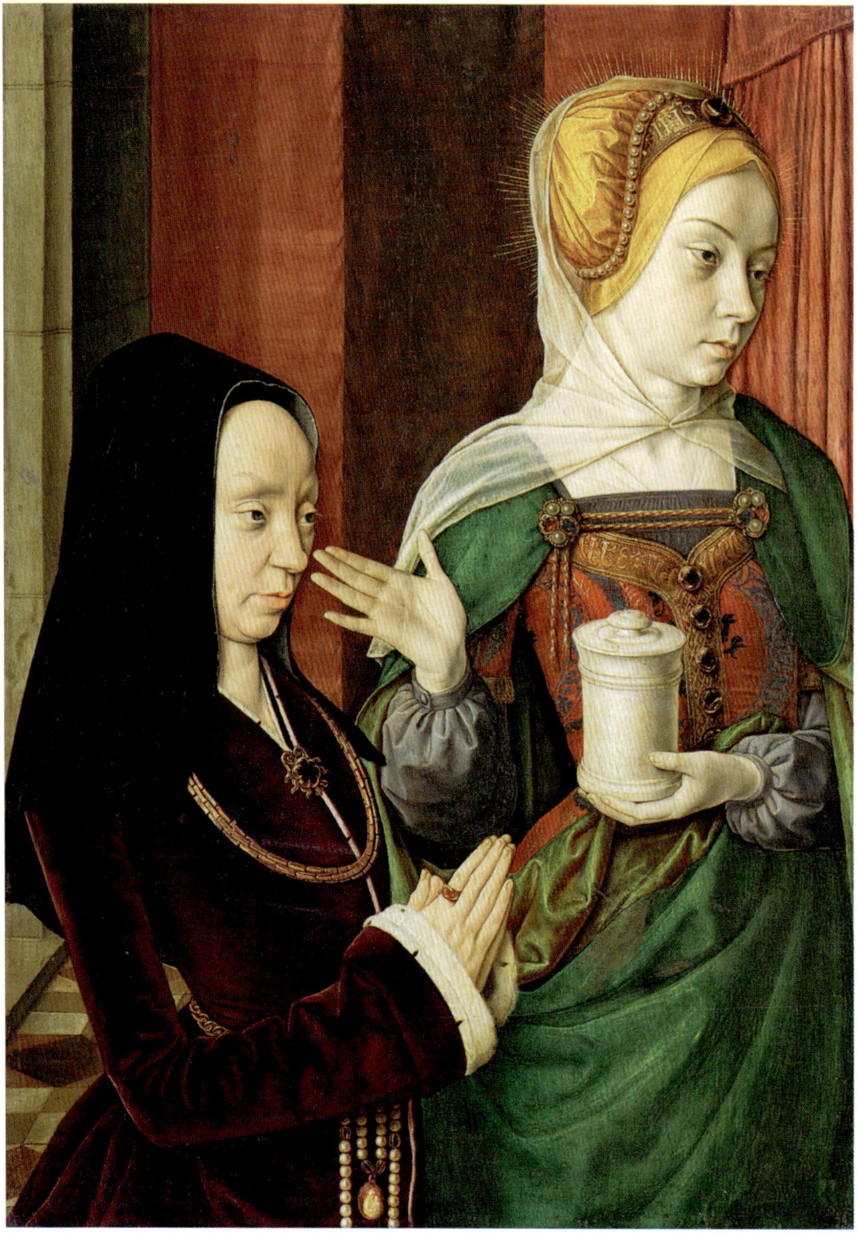

1. **JEAN HEY, *IDENTIFIED WITH THE MAÎTRE DE MOULINS***
(active c. 1472–1504)
Portrait of Madeleine de Bourgogne Presented by Mary Magdalene, c. 1490–1495
Oil on wood, 22 × 15 ¾ in. (56 × 40 cm)

2. **ANONYMOUS**
Clasp, thirteenth century
Silver gilt, pearls, garnets, and sapphires, diam. 2 ½ in. (6 cm)

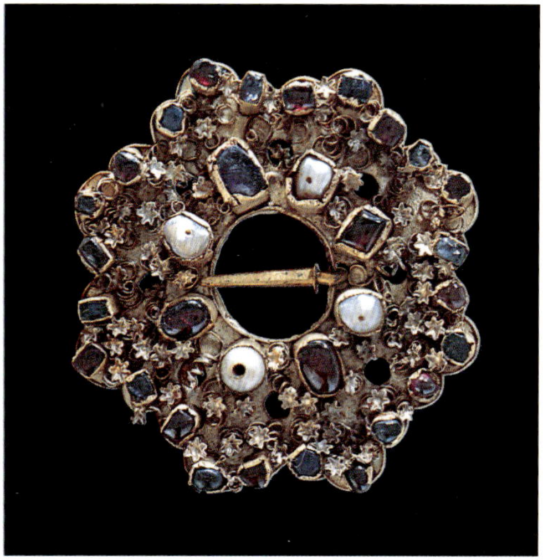

1. It is believed that this painting, the left wing of a diptych or triptych from the end of the fifth century, represents Madeleine de Bourgogne, an illegitimate daughter of the duke of Burgundy, Philip the Good. She is portrayed kneeling, hands clasped, under the protection of her patron saint, Mary Magdalene, who is shown gesturing towards her. The contrast between the stiffness of the mortal model and the grace of the saint is striking. In an attitude of prayer, the former is all humility, seemingly more concerned for her soul than for her earthly appearance. Several signs, however, reveal the fact that Madeleine de Bourgogne, who commissioned the work, was nonetheless a personage of noble origin. The two sections of her ermine-bordered black velvet robe are held together by a fermail brooch. She also displays a large and exquisite gold chain with box links (at this time, each link would have been hammered flat), very different from the one hanging discreetly from her belt, which bears a sheaf of pearls and a religious medallion. The Magdalene, on the other hand, is beautifully and alluringly attired: her hair is adorned with a pearl necklace and two other clasps fixed by chains attach a short cape to her bodice.

2. An ancestor of the ornamental brooch, a *fermail* was a clasp designed to hold together two parts with its *ardillon* (a little pin or tongue). Employed in antiquity especially to fix a piece of clothing draped over the shoulder, the *fermail* was also a medieval jewel that became widespread in the twelfth and thirteenth centuries in many social milieus. The outer ring could take on various forms, round or polyfoil, and was decorated with inscriptions or patterns. Extremely luxurious examples were large and encrusted with diamonds or precious stones. This exceptionally large and elaborate specimen is enriched with pearls, stones, and relief flowerets borne on a tiny *tigella* rolled up into a spiral.

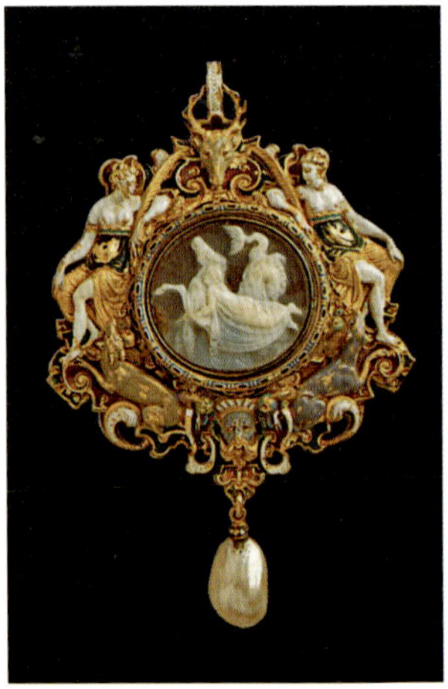

1. ***AFTER FRANÇOIS CLOUET*** (Facing page)
Portrait of Elizabeth of Austria (1554–1592), sixteenth century
Oil on wood, 14 × 10 ¼ in. (36 × 26 cm)

2. **ANONYMOUS**
Pendant decorated with an ancient cameo signed "Sostratos"
Paris, third quarter of the sixteenth century
Cameo on agate, gold, enamel, and pearls, 4 ⅜ × 2 ¾ in. (11 × 7.2 cm)

1. Icon-like and as if frozen in the straitjacket of etiquette, Elizabeth, the wife of the king of France, Charles IX, appears dressed in the at once sumptuous and constricting costume of a sixteenth-century sovereign. The luxuriousness is immediately apparent in the robe, with the sleeves and the upper part of the bodice amply slashed to reveal a gleaming white chemise. The opulence continues in the plethora of stones and pearls adorning the costume: the length of pearls bordering a cap known as a *touret* is taken up by a necklet of pearls and precious stones called a *carcanet*. This is followed by a long necklace, a *cotoire*, bearing a pendant in gold, emeralds, and rubies called a *pentacol*. Pearls and stones are also sewn all around the bodice and close to the slashing. The whole sumptuous ensemble is finished off by a gold-bedecked and bejeweled girdle. For Elizabeth of Austria, however, this would have practically amounted to everyday wear, since at her wedding she had received several complete parures of diamonds, emeralds, pearls, and rubies, all extracted from the newly exploited mines of the New World.

2. From the Middle Ages on, cameos—reliefs cut into agates such as onyx and sardonyx and originally from the ancient world—were collected by the nobility. During the Renaissance, it became customary to mount them on the brooches or pendants that formed an integral part of the resplendent toilettes of the European aristocracy. Italian and French goldsmiths often referred to the designs of *ornemanistes*—pattern-book engravers—for inspiration.

The cameo in the center of this *pentacol*, of unusual size and workmanship, shows a female figure reclining on a hippocampus (amphitrite, perhaps). The engraved stone is ringed with interlacing and with two allegorical enamel figures, as well as a pair of greyhounds, symbols of fidelity. The stag's head atop the piece, symbol of Diane de Poitiers, suggests the jewel might have once belonged to her. The quality of the piece is such that it is generally attributed to Étienne Delaune (1518–1583), a celebrated stone graver who worked at the French court between 1546 and 1572.

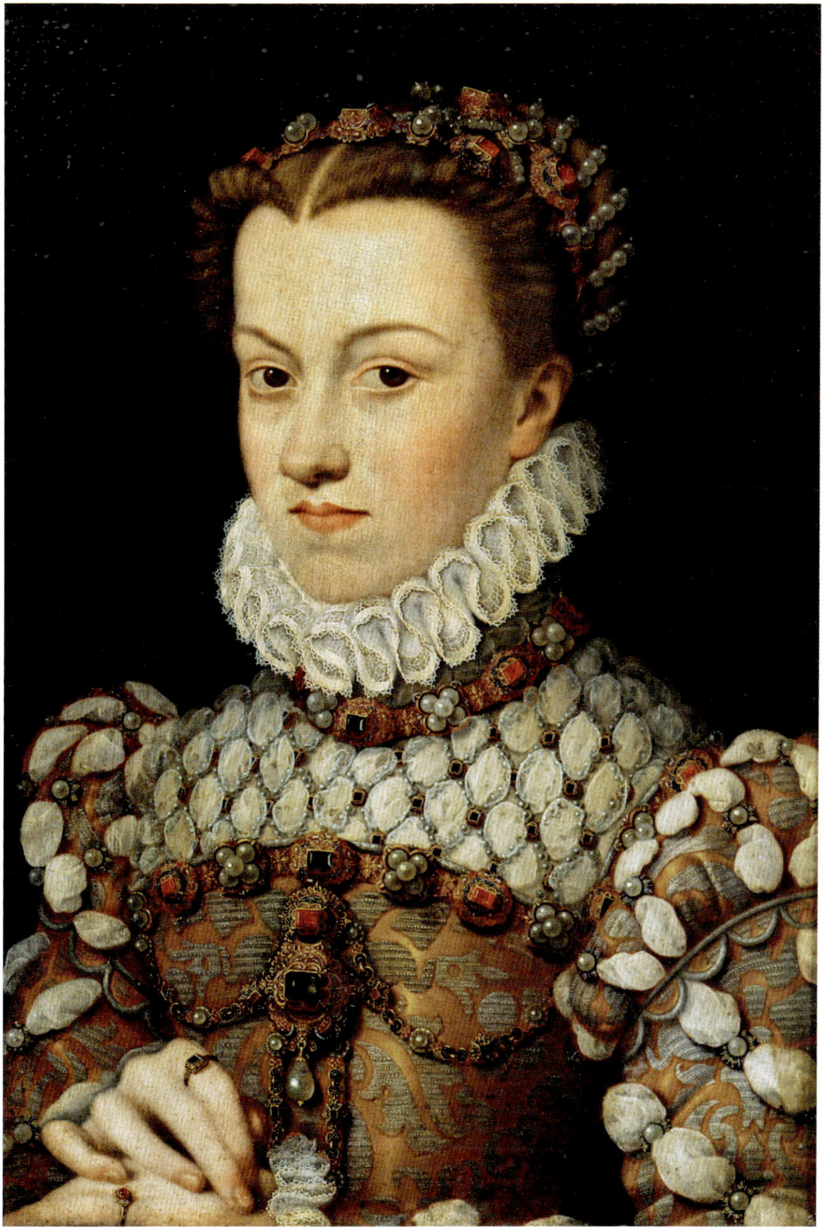

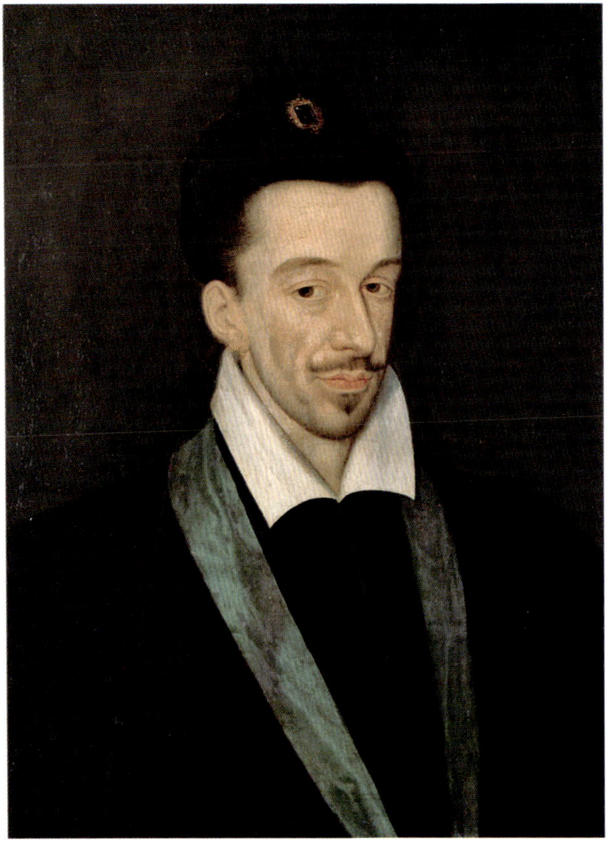

***ATTRIBUTED TO* FRANÇOIS QUESNEL** (1543–1616)
Henry III King of France, c. 1582–1586
Oil on wood, 26 × 20 ½ in. (66 × 52 cm)

This austere portrait of Henry III of France does not conform to his reputation as a somewhat effeminate sovereign. The poet Agrippa d'Aubigné dubbed him the *roy-femme* or *homme-reyne*—"king-woman" or "man-queen." A satire of the time amplifies the king's hybrid moniker: "The *demy-femme* was brought a small box in which there were many rings; he chose some of them and these were placed on his fingers; he then ordered a tiny jewel-case to be fetched from which two pendants were extracted and hung onto his ears and then a small chain of pearls interwoven with figures that was put on his arm. Another great chain was brought and placed over his neck." Everything in this text conspires to present the monarch as excessively mannered, and he did indeed like to make up and powder his face and surround himself with youthful minions. However, during the Renaissance courtiers generally were fond of wearing rings and in this respect Henry III was not exceptional. Hairstyles left the ears uncovered so as to expose the fashionable large earrings. Although dressed soberly in this portrait, in what was considered the Spanish mode, with a toque, decorated with a jewel surmounted by an aigrette, the king also wears a number of earrings in his right ear (piercing clearly is no modern fad). The long blue ribbon visible on the king's chest most probably bears the insignia of the Order of the Holy Spirit, which the sovereign himself had instituted in 1578.

AFTER **ANDREA SOLARIO** (c. 1465–1524)
Portrait of Charles d'Amboise, c. 1507
Oil on wood, 29 ½ × 20 ½ in. (75 × 52 cm)

In the sixteenth century, pride and the desire for personal prestige led princes to commission portraits of themselves in an as imposing manner as possible. Although idealized, these portraits nonetheless amount to a mine of information for the historian of costume and personal adornment, as illustrated by this portrait of Charles d'Amboise. As French governor to Milan during the reign of Louis XII, it was incumbent upon him to appear in all the dignity of his rank. He is represented half-length, slightly in profile, luxuriously garbed in a coat whose intentionally gaping armholes reveal ample silk-brocade sleeves underneath. His cap is decorated with an emblem that started life as a humble pilgrim badge but which over time became an item of secular jewelry. The impressive neck-chain is from the Order of St Michael, a chivalric order instituted by Louis XI in 1469 and lasting until 1830 when it was disbanded by Louis-Philippe. Each member wore a gold necklace made of shells (also a pilgrim's symbol) held together by knots of double aglets. The central section bore an enamel medallion representing St. Michael slaying the devil in the form of a dragon. In 1516, Francis I had the neck-chain modified, replacing the aglets with a double strand of gold cording. To be a knight of the Order of St. Michael was an honor, but it had its duties, too. In public the great neck-chain had to be draped over the clothing, but for less formal occasions a simple ribbon with the saint's effigy sufficed.

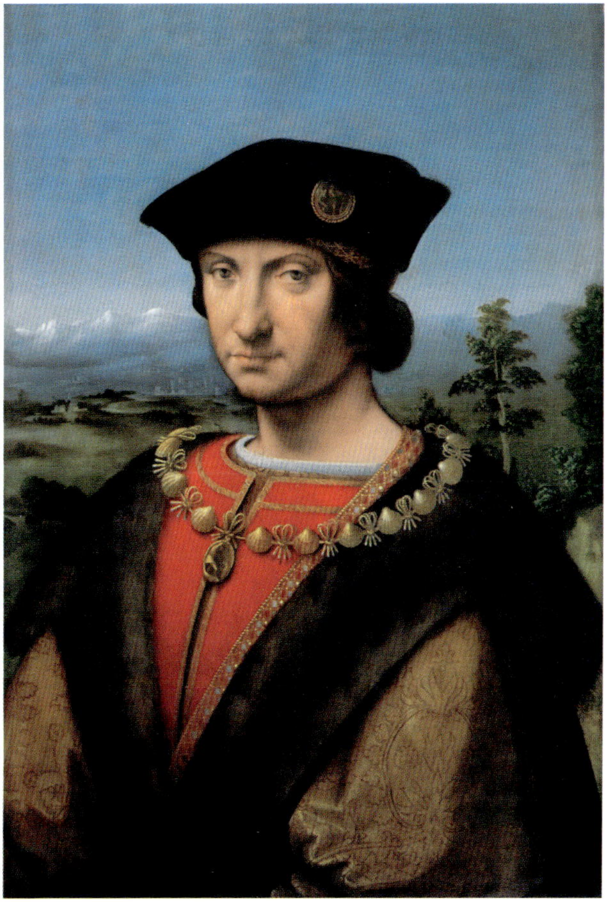

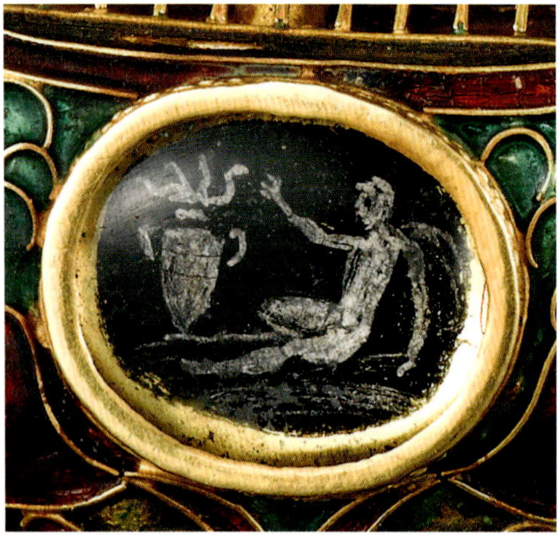

ANONYMOUS
Pendant in the shape of a ship
Italy (?), second half of the sixteenth century
Enameled gold, pearls, and paint under crystal, 4 × 2 ⅜ in. (10.3 × 5.9 cm)

In the second half of the sixteenth century, jewelers, responding to the ever more refined taste of their patrons, began producing miniature masterpieces of goldwork in the form of pendants combining precious stones with pearls and enamel. Inspired by classical antiquity, the decorative repertory took on a new lease of life. Jewelry was decorated with nymphs and goddesses as well as more whimsical forms, such as boats reminiscent of both the caravels that were then setting out for the New World and nefs—those boat-shaped silverwork centerpieces that graced the dining tables of the nobility. These "little ships" were enlivened with amusing allegorical scenes allowing the enameler to display his technical prowess.

This one has a full sail billowing in the wind, a mast rigged with shrouds spun with pearls, and, at the poop, a little wheelhouse—the aftercastle—as well as a stem-post at the prow. The hull, worked into fish-scales, is set in the center with an oval medallion in *verre églomisé,* or gilded glass. The pendant and the little suspension chains are dotted with baroques—that is, as the term originally meant, misshapen pearls.

Much prized in the Mannerist period, jewels in the shape of watercraft were given as engagement or wedding presents. In this context they symbolized the storms of love, but they were also adopted as ex-votos to protect against flooding.

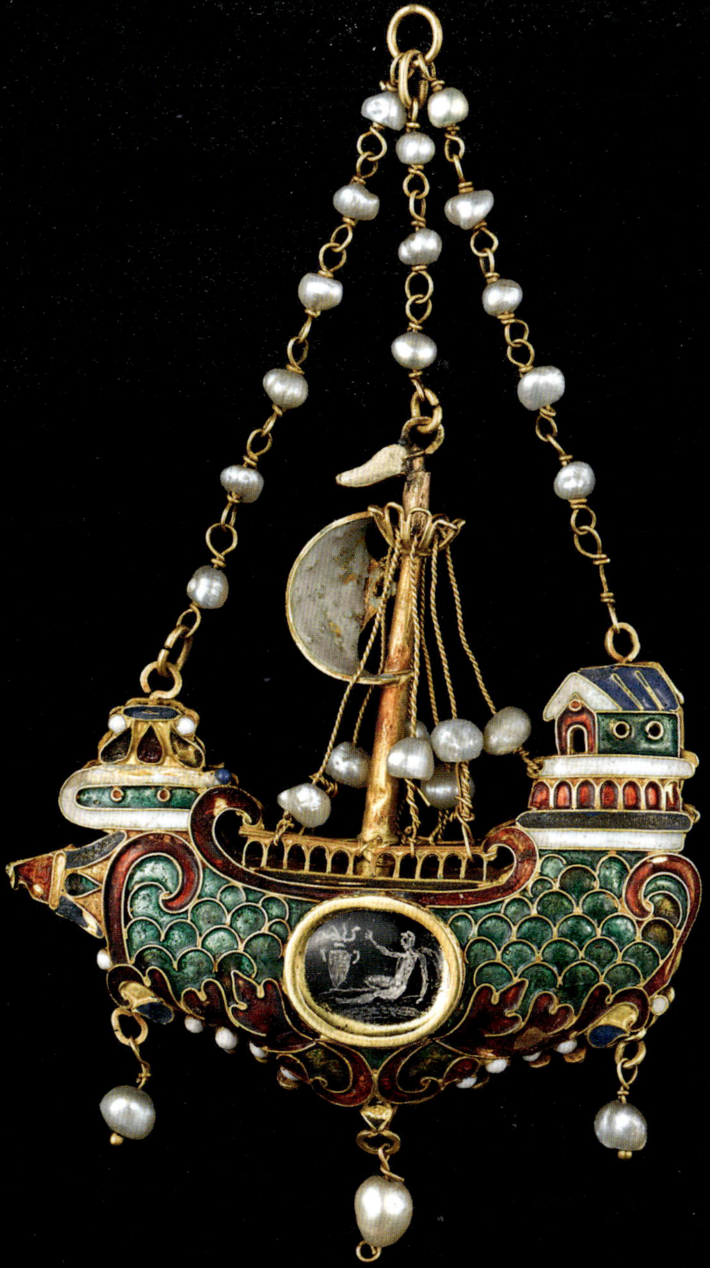

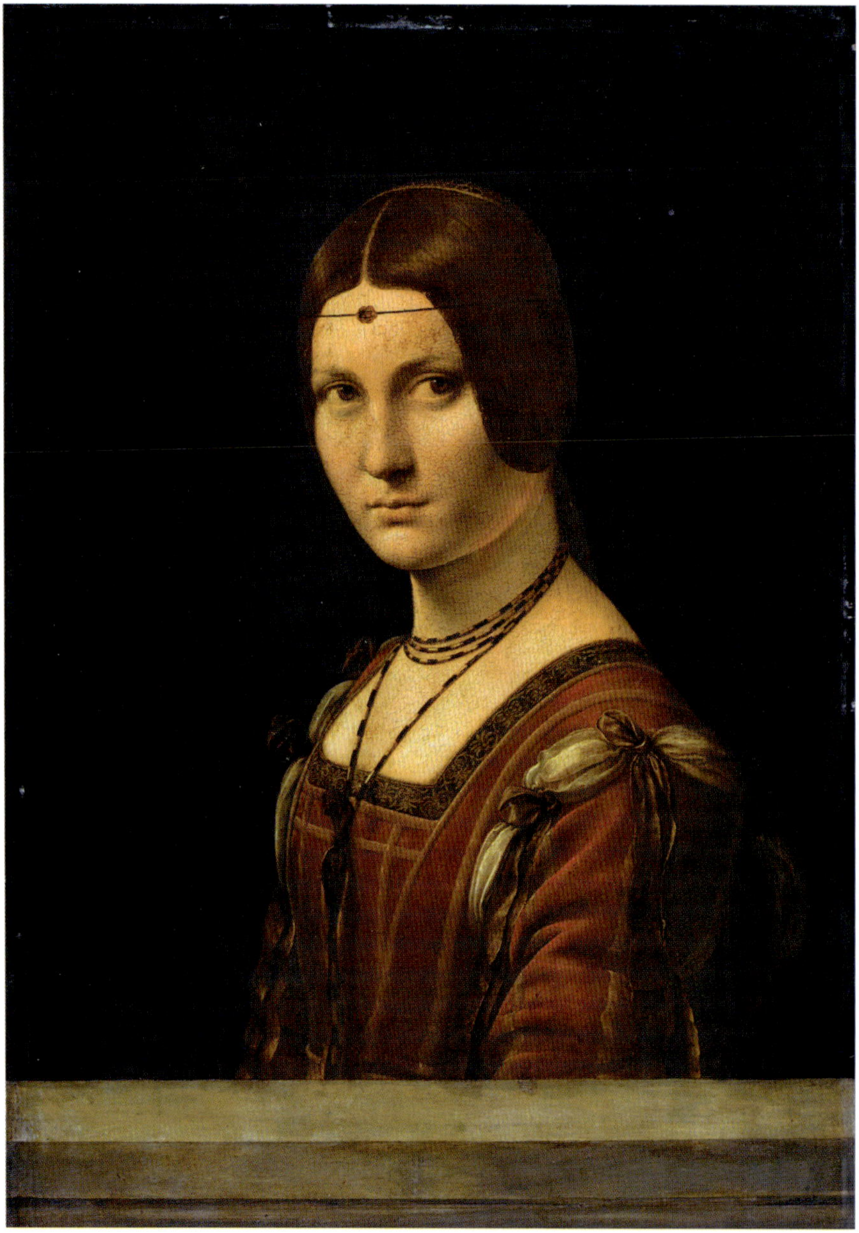

1. **LEONARDO DA VINCI** (1452–1519)
Portrait of a Lady (La Belle Ferronnière), 1592
Oil on wood, 24 ¾ × 17 ¾ in. (63 × 45 cm)

2. **JEAN-BAPTISTE CAMILLE COROT** (1796–1875)
Woman with a Pearl (La Femme à la perle), c. 1868
Oil on canvas, 30 × 17 ½ in. (70 × 55 cm)

It has been a subject of fierce debate whether this portrait (I), which is believed to be of Lucrezia Crivelli, one of the mistresses of Ludovico Sforzo (known as Il Moro, "the Moor"), Duke of Milan, is entirely by Leonardo. The mystery of the painting is further complicated by its title, since it was perhaps borrowed from another portrait that represented a mistress of Francis I, also known as La Belle Feronnière. In any event, this young woman does indeed possess the mysterious distinction and beauty characteristic of many of Leonardo da Vinci's portraits.

Her perfect oval face is ringed in a hairstyle dressed with bands that hide her ears but reveal a feathery net on the back of her head that extends over a lock of hair. A four-rowed necklace gracing the low neckline is comprised of tubular beads that are hard to identify: are they made of gold and jet, a form of lignite, then very costly, or are they of the hand-painted *pâte de verre* in which Venice then excelled? The jewel adorning the figure's forehead is an innovation—a length of fine gold wire with a stone in the center.

In 1752 this was described by the painter Lépicié as "a black braid with a diamond in the middle." This decoration, also known as a *ferronnière*, came back into fashion in the nineteenth century, along with the "Troubadour" style that was promoted most notably by the Duchess of Berry around 1830. The *Belle Ferronnière* herself reappears as the model for Camille Corot's portrait *The Woman with a Pearl.*

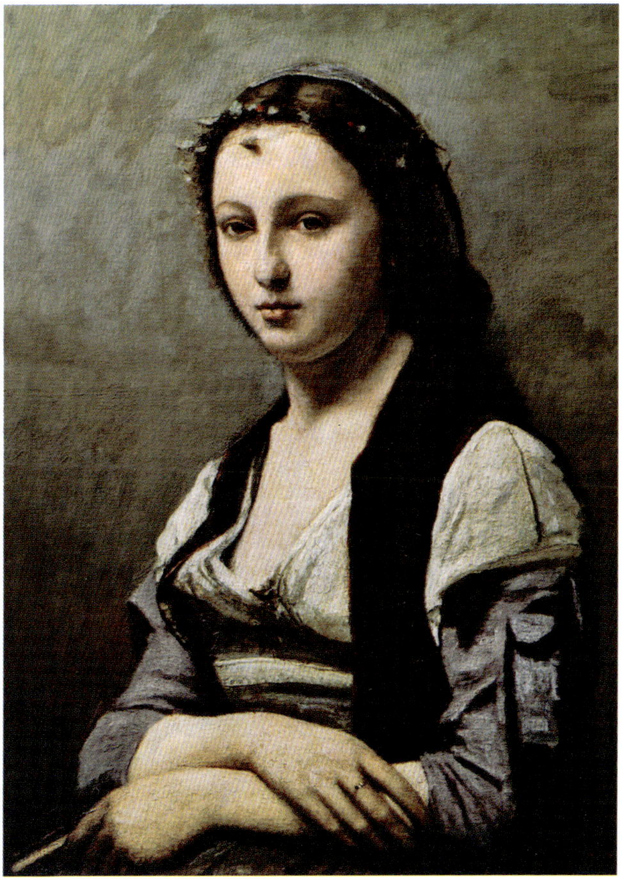

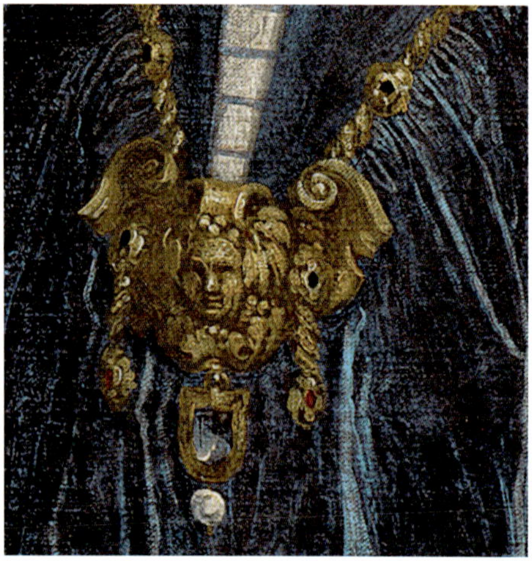

PAOLO CALIARI, *CALLED* VERONESE (1528–1588)
Venetian Lady known as *La Bella Nani*, c. 1560
Oil on canvas, 3 ft. 10 ¾ in. × 3 ft. 4 ½ in. (1.19 × 1.03 m)

During the Renaissance, pearls brought back from the Americas by the Conquistadores became a new source of wealth, but they remained a luxury, and in Venice a trade in imitation pearls flourished. An ever-present accessory of aristocratic attire, threaded pearls were worn round the lower part of the neck, generally in a single row. They became so abundant on clothing that many edicts in Europe attempted, without success, to limit their use. The sixteenth century could indeed be called the Golden Age of the pearl.

The costume of La Bella Nani—a beauty whose identity has never been firmly established—is a veritable catalogue of sixteenth-century Venetian personal adornment, including, of course, jewelry, such as the necklace of large round pearls, and the pearl-adorned hairstyle. The fashion for fine cauls bedecked with pearls, so popular in the first half of the century, was no longer de rigueur, and pearls were now braided directly into the hair. The robe is discreetly set off by a chain of gold, bracelets, and a golden girdle. As garment adornments, the larger pieces in the shape of female masks placed at the bottom of the bodice and on the shoulders attaching the veil are exceptional, and derive more from the decorative repertory of the silversmith than of the jeweler in the strict sense. As the technique of engraving developed, many pattern-books for the use of embroiderers, goldsmiths, and sculptors started to appear, and it is conceivable that Veronese referred to one of these—unless, that is, they sprung fully fledged from his imagination.

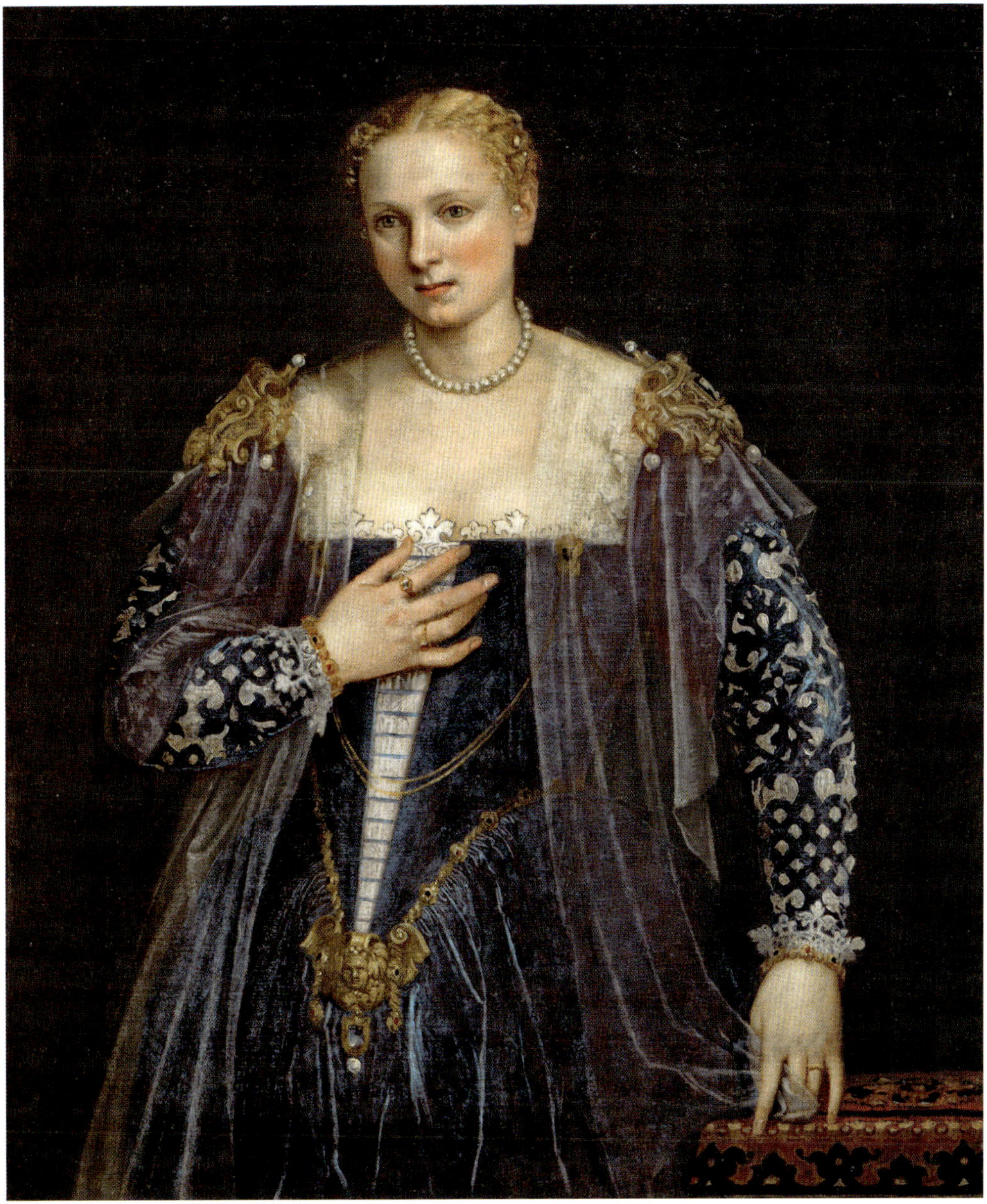

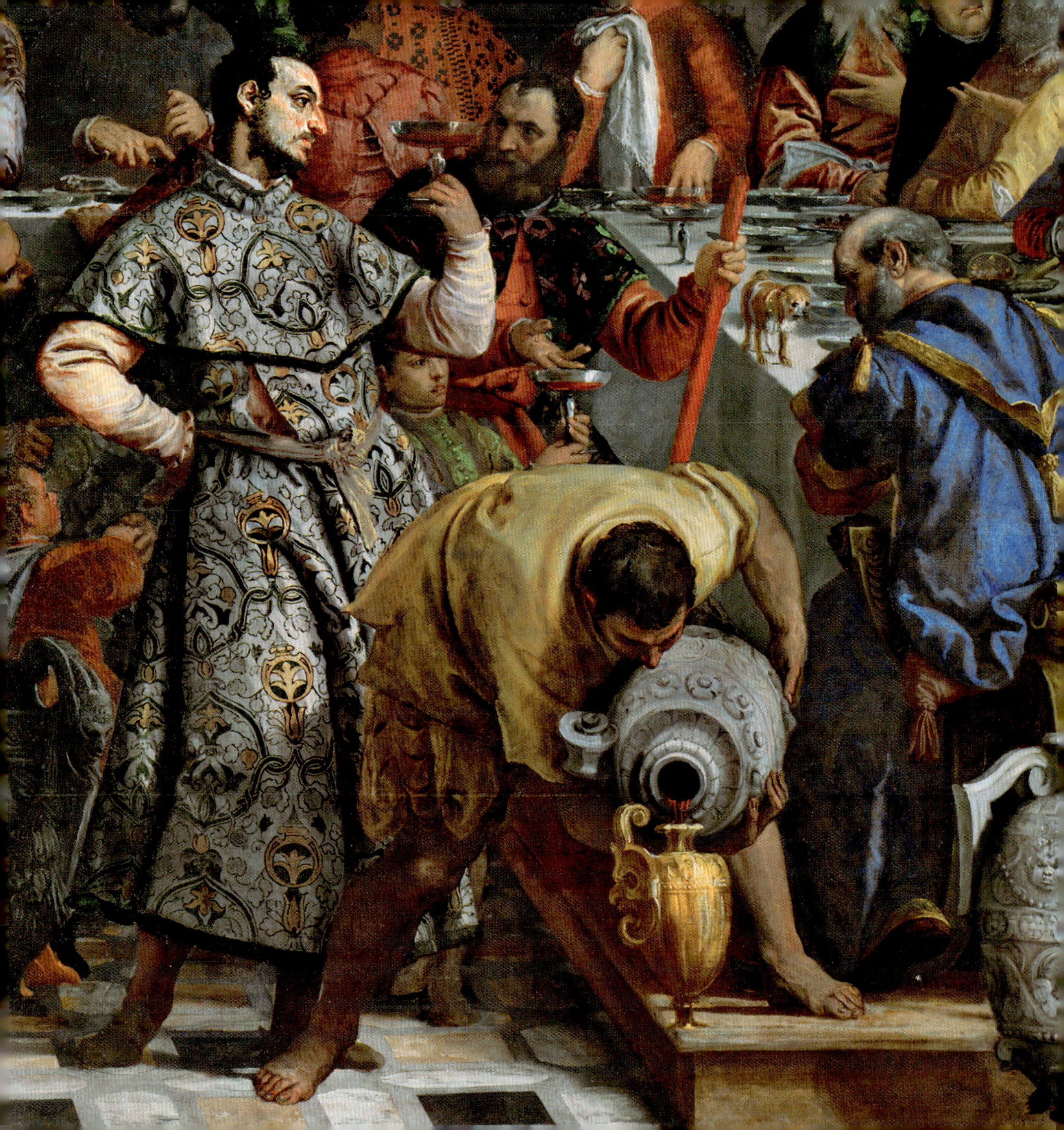

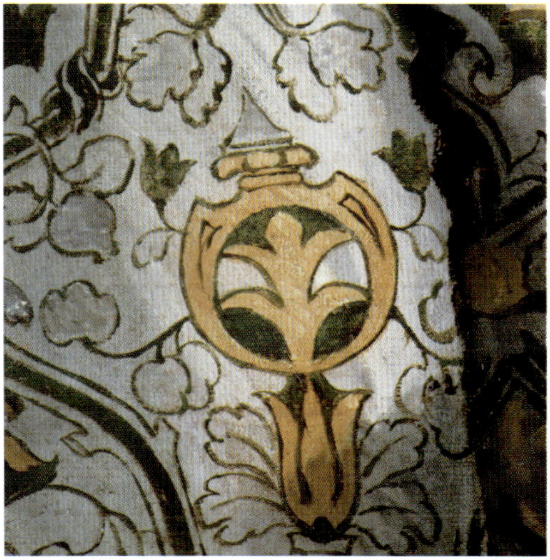

PAOLO CALIARI, ***CALLED*** **VERONESE** (1528–1588)
The Wedding at Cana, 1562–1564
Oil on canvas, 12 ft. 2 ½ in. × 32 ft. 7 ⅜ in. (6.77 × 9.94 m)

Veronese chose to portray the meal at the wedding in Cana from the Gospels as a wedding feast such as might have been held in mid-sixteenth-century Venice. All the women present, beginning with the bride, wear the ostentatious dress and opulent jewelry of contemporary Venetian society. Although perhaps less noticeable at first glance, the dress of the cup-bearer, too, is highly revealing. The fabric is decorated with a ring from which springs an open tulip, a symbol of marriage and fruitfulness, and thus an appropriate motif for the painting. This kind of ring, here associated with a wedding band, seldom appears on textiles, although an earlier example can be found on the robe of Semiramis in Botticelli's of *Pallas and the Centaur*, painted in about 1480. The decorative motif is an insignia of Lorenzo the Magnificent (1449–1492), who commissioned Botticelli's painting. The source for Veronese's cup-bearer, however, is a miniature representing, in idealized fashion, the wedding of Costanzo Sforza and Camilla d'Aragona in 1475, now in the Vatican Library, Rome. It depicts the allegorical figure of Hymen wearing a garment identical to that of the cup-bearer. Here, however, the fabric is adorned with a ring whose diamond, also cut to a point, frames two blazing torches. The accompanying commentary runs: "Two torches in a ring of burning fire/Two wills, two hearts, two passions/Joined in marriage by a diamond."

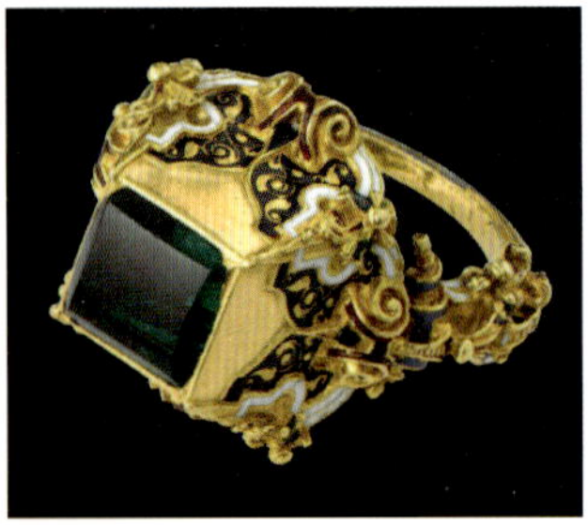

1. **HANS HOLBEIN, *CALLED* THE YOUNGER** (1497–1543) (Facing page)
Portrait of Anne of Cleves, 1539
Oil on parchment, 25 ½ × 18 in (65 × 46 cm)

2. **ANONYMOUS**
Ring, Italy, sixteenth century,
Gold enamel and emerald, d. 1 ¼ in. (3.2 cm)

1. For his fourth wife, the powerful and much-feared king Henry VIII—who had already divorced the first (Catherine of Aragon), had the second (Anne Boleyn) executed, and lost the third (Jane Seymour) in childbirth—set his heart on a German princess, Anne of Cleves, and ordered a portrait from his painter by appointment, who carried it out at the prospective wife's court during the summer of 1539. The artist paints a portrait of a rather plain woman, who gazes out impassively, but he accurately reproduces the dazzling costume of the young woman, her hair set in the German fashion, and entirely concealed beneath a caul comprising a lattice of pearls and a bolt of muslin. The robe and coat, trimmed with braiding known as galloons, are sewn with pearl buttons and enameled gold cabochons. The square décolleté is adorned with a necklace and two chains. A cross made of diamond roses with a pearl at their heart hangs from an elaborate, close-fitting necklace. The longer gold chains consist of cylindrical links, less common than round or filed wire rings. Her crossed hands also show off a number of rings. At their first meeting, however, this fine attire—similar to what Henry VIII himself wore—was not sufficient to win over the king. Not only was Anne's face pockmarked, but the king found her too tall and is alleged to have compared her to "a Flanders mare." Nonetheless, in 1540, he wed the princess, only to repudiate her a few months later: an enviable enough fate compared to that of his next victim, Catherine Howard, who was to lose her head.

2. Whether it was because they were slaves to fashion or lovers of display, portraits of Renaissance men and women reveal that they wore several rings on their thumbs, as well as their index and middle fingers. The beautifully worked one presented here is in the shape of a circular band adorned with scrolls and florets. The flat, table-cut emerald in the bezel is encircled by gold enamel volutes. During this period, only two types of cut were employed for stones: point- and table-cut. An emerald, from Peru or India, was only marginally less valuable than a ruby, and it had to be worked with meticulous care to get the most out of it. "One should," wrote the great goldsmith and sculptor Benvenuto Cellini (1515–1557), "neither set it too deep—this obscures its value—nor too high, as that isolates it from the surrounding details." The designer of this ring has taken these rules to heart.

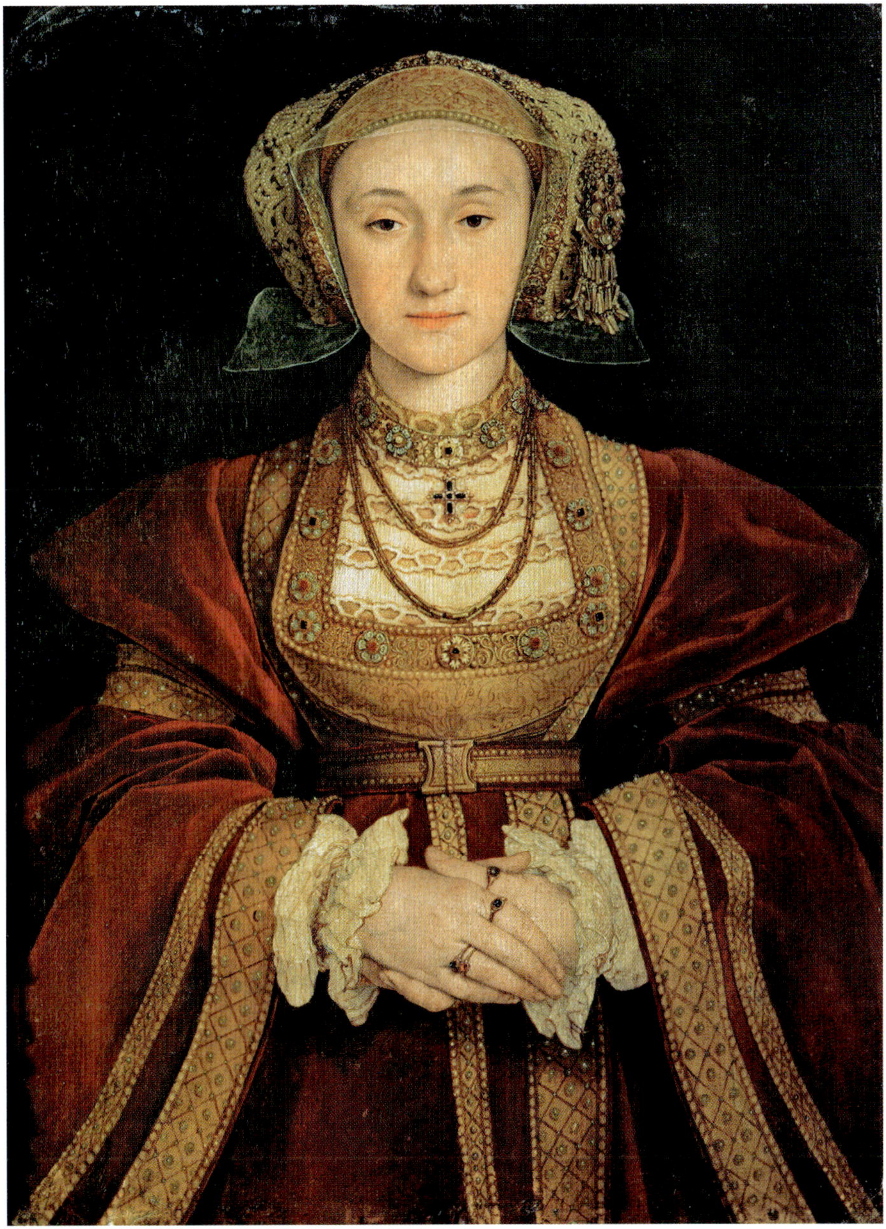

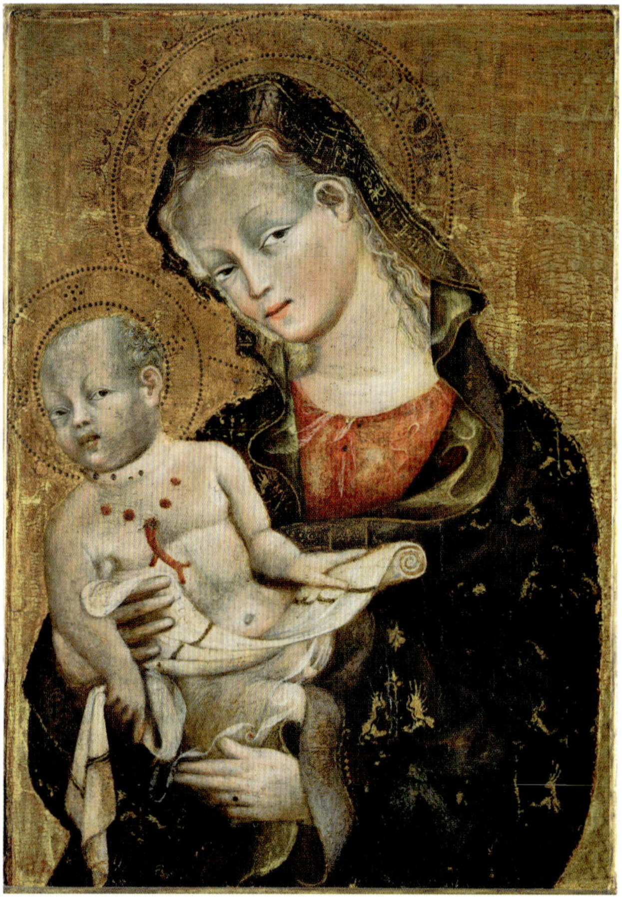

GIOVANNI DA MODENA (active c. 1398–1456)
Virgin and Child, beginning of the fifteenth century
Oil on wood, 25 ¼ × 17 ¾ in. (64 × 45 cm)

Many Renaissance depictions of the Virgin and Child show the infant Christ wearing a coral necklace with a pendant. In former times, illness posed a significant threat to newborns and toddlers, and more than any other baby, Jesus had to be protected. In the absence of any truly effective medical treatment, many elements from the mineral and plant worlds were applied to the body in the hope they might forestall or even cure ailments. One such prophylactic was coral. Retrieved from the bottom of the sea, according to ancient legend it was thought to have congealed from drops of blood from Medusa, one of the three Gorgons beheaded by Perseus. Coral was popularly believed to ward off the Evil Eye and it was combined with amulets made in other materials to make pendants. Because of its color, red coral was meant to halt hemorrhaging, while its twisted branches were meant to help in the treatment of the internal organs.

ANONYMOUS
Pectoral cross, second third of the sixteenth century
Enameled gold, rock crystal, and pearls, 2 ⅞ × 1 ¾ in.
(7.4 × 4.5 cm)

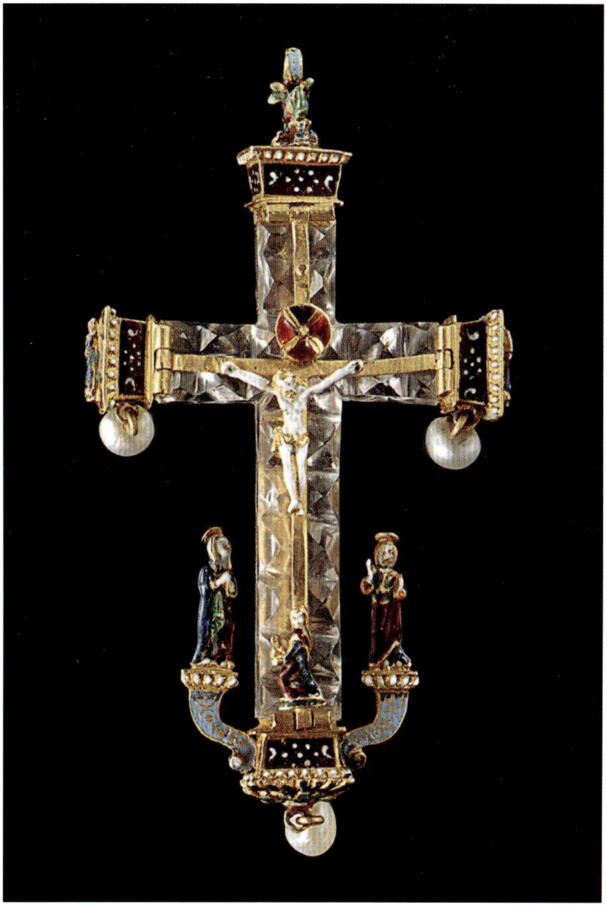

This beautifully bright, rock-crystal cross displays various Christian symbols of love and suffering: Christ on the Cross, surmounted by a pelican, with Mary Magdalene at his feet and, to either side, St. John and the Virgin Mary. The cross is naturally the most important article of devotional jewelry, as a representation of Jesus' martyrdom. It can appear in many guises, with the equal-armed Greek cross found in some Protestant churches, while the Latin variety, with its shorter arms, is more prevalent among Catholics. Like almost all religious insignia of this time, this cross was sewn to cloth, and would then be hung round the neck. Regarded as a jewel, a cross did not necessarily feature Christ and the Virgin: it could be made out of filigree metal, enameled and covered in pearls or gems, or more simply in engraved gold. In the sixteenth century, crosses fixed to the ends of a chain or necklace were generally made of gold and precious stones. Rarer, cut-crystal examples with arms terminating in an ornament in gold enamel generally originated in Lombardy or Spain, sites of famous workshops in the sixteenth and seventeenth centuries. In Christian symbolism, the pearls that set off the jewel so prettily were emblematic of Christ and of his virgin birth.

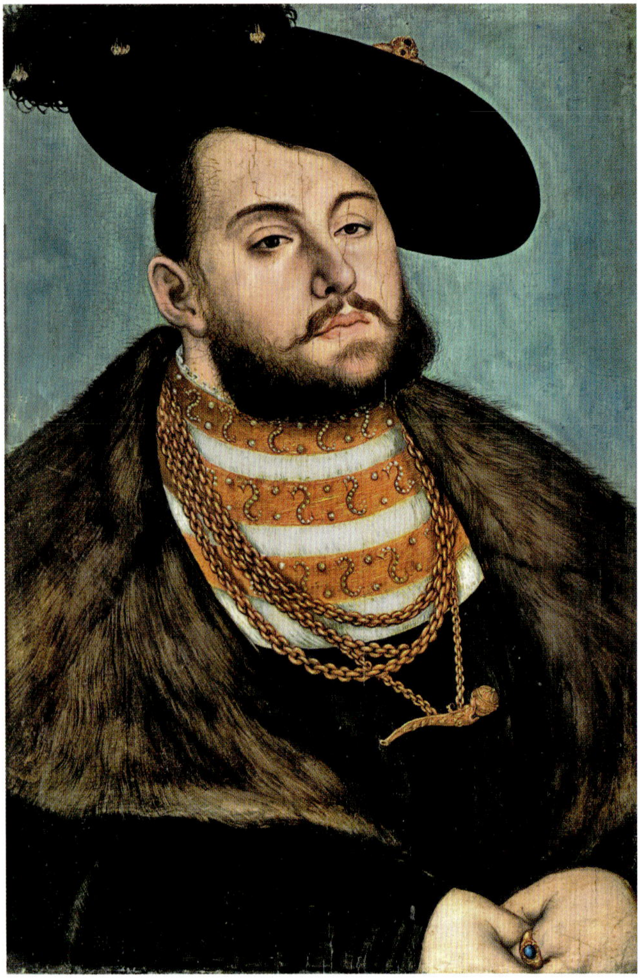

LUCAS CRANACH THE ELDER
(1472–1553)
Portrait of John Frederick, the Magnanimous, Elector of Saxony, 1531
Oil on wood, 25 ¼ × 16 ½ in. (64 × 42 cm)

The allure of this German elector is that of a typical sixteenth-century lord. His hat, at a mildly rakish angle, is sewn with three gold pins, a head ornament adopted by every European prince. The enormous, wide-necked greatcoat (or *chamarre*) emphasizes the quadruple chain. The fashion for chains and necklaces dates from the fifteenth century, when a woman would display them ostentatiously at her décolleté or a man on his chest. Moreover, kings and emperors began the practice of bestowing gold chains as a sign of their favor. (In the eighteenth century, this function as a token of regard and gratitude was to be usurped by the snuffbox.) The object suspended from one of the chains of the Crown Prince of Saxony is not strictly a jewel; it is rather a piece of goldwork, which might be an elaborate ear-pick (that might have doubled as a toothpick), although closer examination suggests it is more likely to be a whistle in the form of a dolphin with a perfume apple in its mouth. Small pendants containing sweet-smelling fragrances were common in the Renaissance. Still, like other scented accoutrements, precious articles such as these wrought by silversmiths and worn at the end of a chain on the chest or the belt, possess all the grace of true jewelry.

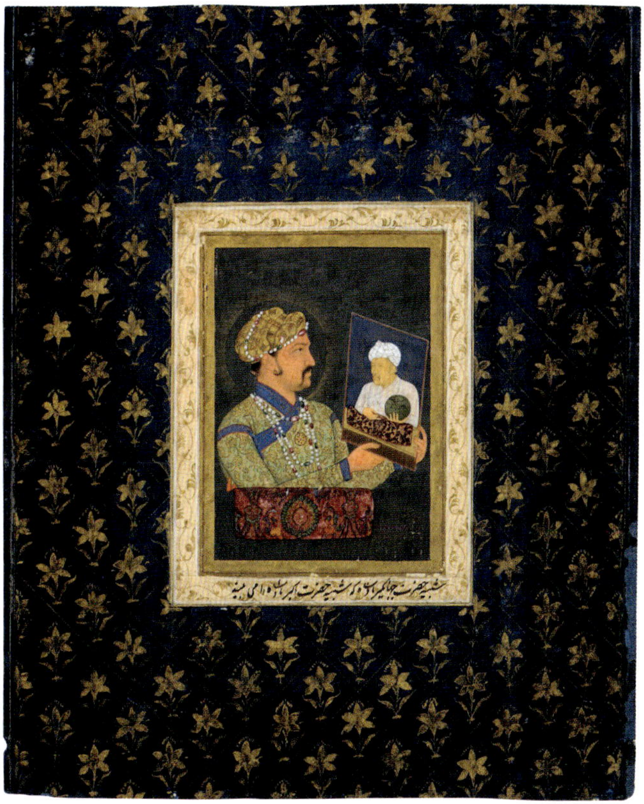

ABU'L HASAN NADIR AR-ZAMAN *AND* HASHIM
Djahangir Holding a Portrait of his Father, Emperor Akbar, India, c. 1605
Miniature on paper with gouache and gold, 7 ¼ × 4 ½ in. (18.3 × 11.6 cm)

During the period of Akbar (1542–1605) and his elder son Jahangir (1569–1624), the Mughal dynasty (1526–1857), which was to rule India from the sixteenth to the nineteenth century, experienced an era of prosperity and artistic creativity, in which jewelry of an extreme refinement held pride of place. Princes and sovereigns were fond of complex and elaborate adornments and enjoyed jewelry drenched in vast quantities of fine pearls from the Persian Gulf, as well as gemstones extracted from the numerous Indian mines. The pleasure of possessing and displaying such jewels was compounded by widespread veneration for gems, which were universally believed to act as prophylactics and cures for illnesses. According to Indian tradition, all precious stones could be of beneficial influence to the human body. Seed pearls were thrown over the Maharajah at his crowning by well-wishers, topaz was thought to prevent sleepwalking, the diamond—called a "piece of eternity"—served as a defense against mishap, while the ruby, the "lord of precious stones" and symbol of love, was the most vaunted due to its radiant power.

With his turban and caftan decorated with rivers of pearls and emeralds, Jahangir, the Mughal sovereign, must surely have been more than adequately protected. Nonetheless, his appearance is relatively sober compared to the splendidly attired Maharajahs we see in photographs from the beginning of the twentieth century, who seem literally encased in pearls and jewels.

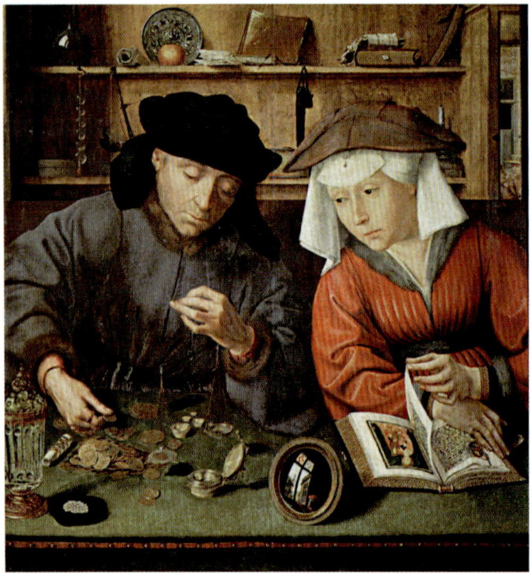

QUENTIN METSYS (1466–1530)
The Moneylender and his Wife, 1514
Oil on wood, 28 × 26 ¾ in. (71 × 68 cm)

In the fifteenth and sixteenth centuries, Flemish society benefited from a significant middle class comprised of merchants and craftsmen. Although recently enriched thanks to the cloth trade, they nonetheless preferred being depicted in comparatively homely settings. The jewelers' and goldsmiths' guild was a powerful one, as this couple amply illustrates. This painting has been known variously as *the Goldweigher, Jewelry Merchant*, *Moneychanger* or even *Miser and his Wife*—all the interpretations are equally valid. Whereas the young woman's sole jewel is a gold pin retaining the front flap of her cap, the eye is drawn to the still life on the left, with its heap of gold coins, bag of pearls, scales, and pile of cup-weights, with others scattered over the table. The jeweler employs these tools in essaying and valuing the various materials used in making rings; indeed several examples of the finished article can be seen fitted over a roll of paperboard that serves as a ring-holder. Such rings recall several portraits from the same period showing men flashing one or more rings on their fingers or in their hands. Such a gesture might refer to the occupation of the sitter—goldsmith or jeweler—or might signal his attachment to his late wife.

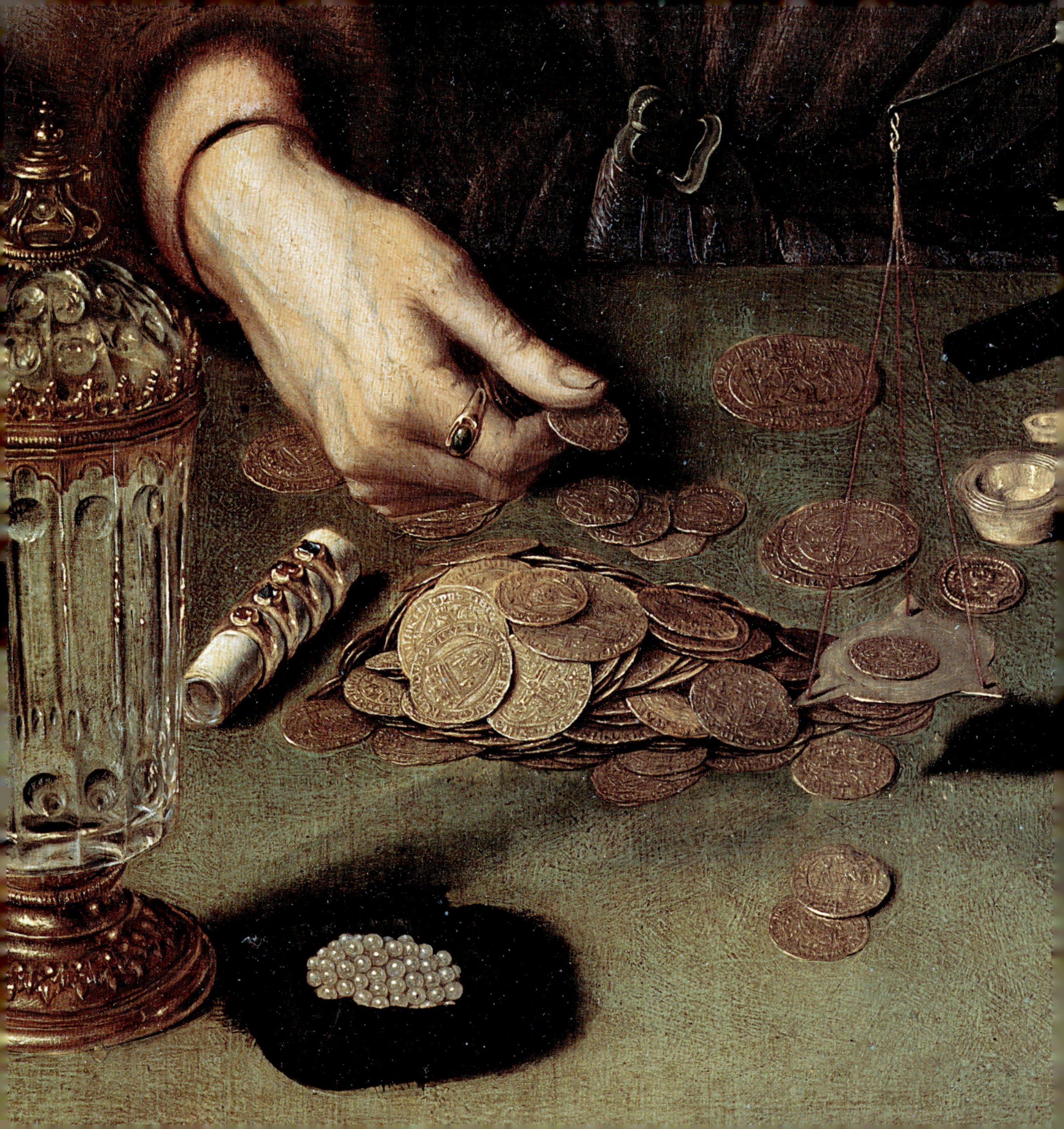

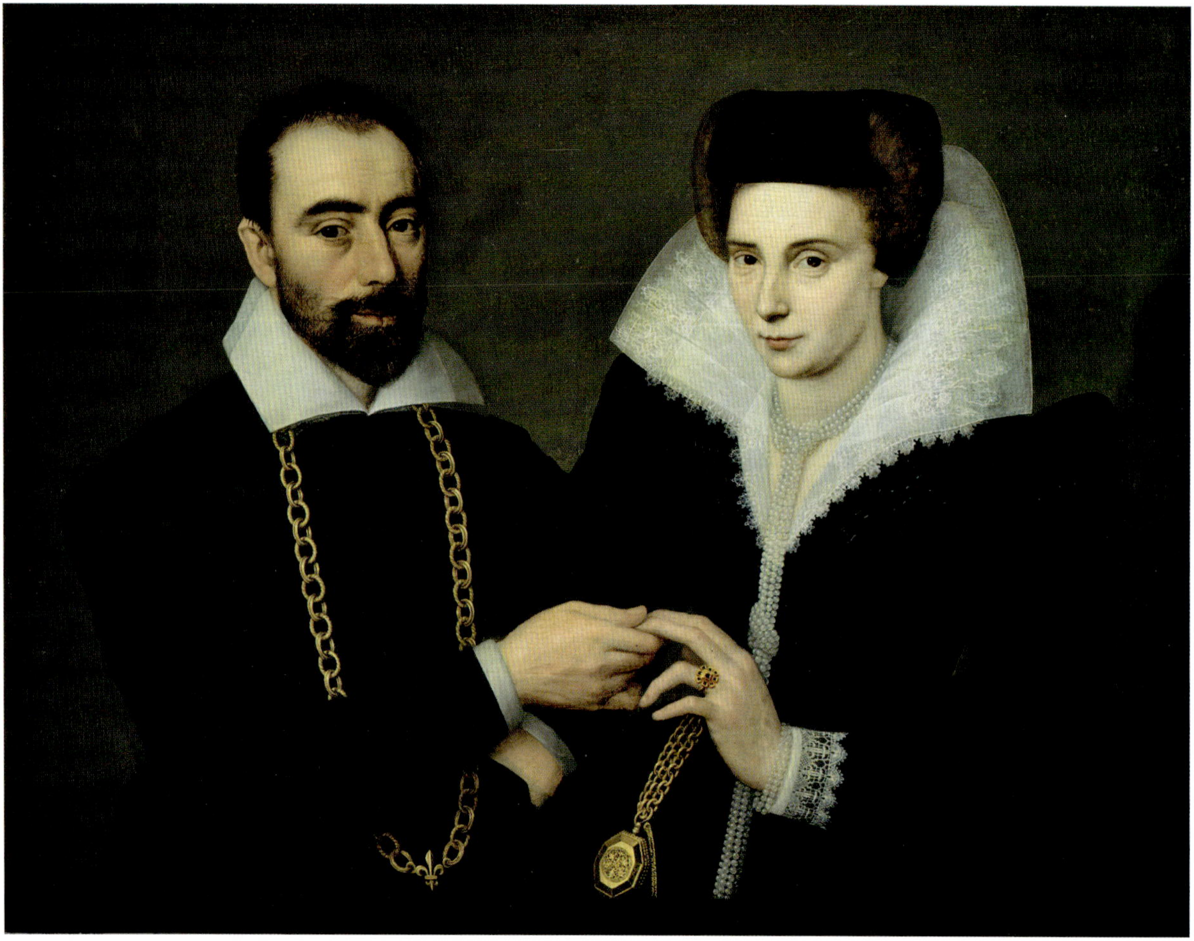

1. FRENCH SCHOOL
Double portrait
Early seventeenth century
Oil on wood, 28 ¾ × 37 ¾ in. (73 × 96 cm)

2. CLAUDE CHAMPAGNEUX *OR* CHAMPAGNIEU, watchmaker
Octagonal watch
Lyon, second quarter of the seventeenth century
Rock crystal and brass, 2 × 1 ¼ × ⅞ in.
(5.2 × 3.1 × 2.3 cm)

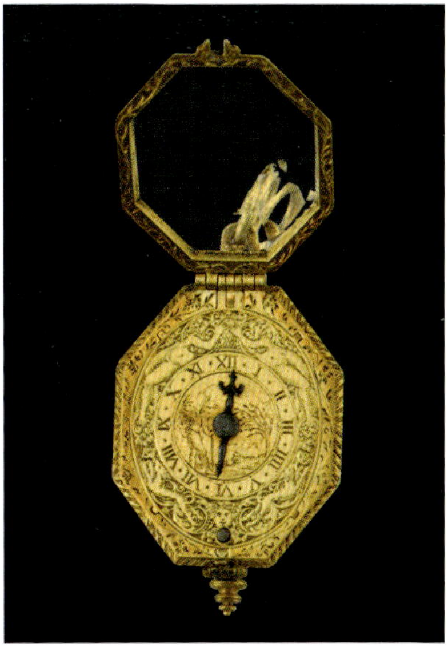

1. The portrait was a pictorial genre that developed in Europe from the sixteenth century onward, above all in middle-class milieus. As Giorgio Vasari (1511–1574), celebrated author of the *Lives of the Artists* wrote: "It became customary in this city [Venice] for men of any importance to have his portrait painted either by Giovanni [Bellini] or some other." Such likenesses might also be painted in commemoration of some event in the individual's life—such as a betrothal, wedding or birthday—as suggested here by the gestures and attitudes of this couple. The man, who has already slipped a band over his wife's left ring-finger, still holds three fingers of her hand as a sign of their union. In their eyes the moment was significant enough to be fixed for all eternity. The austere costumes and discreetly sumptuous jewelry indicate that this couple was probably well-off gentry; or perhaps better than well-off, since the man's chain, made of simple links, terminates in a fleur de lis. The octagonal watch suspended from the chain hanging at the lady's belt was a rarity until the beginning of the seventeenth century.

2. The first "pocket" watches of a size to be carried comfortably were produced at the beginning of the sixteenth century. At the outset they only marked the hours, the minutes being a subsequent development; only later would they sound the hours and play tunes. Scarce and expensive, watches were generally hung round the neck or from a belt in full view. Through the crystal case—oval, octagonal, or in the shape of cross—one could consult, as with this example, a brass dial engraved with allegorical figures and inscribed with an hour circle. A single hand, made in blued steel, signals the hours. The customary three-movement watch, which Antoine Furetière's celebrated dictionary (1619–1688) dubbed the "drunkard's watch" because it could be wound up in either direction, dates only from the mid-seventeenth century.

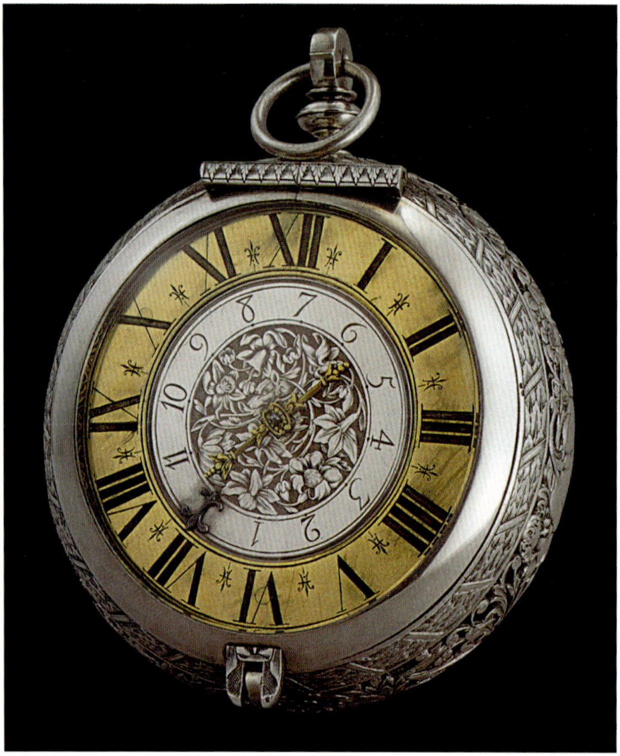

FRANÇOIS DE HECQ, watchmaker
Carriage watch with the coat-of-arms of Cardinal Richelieu
Orleans, c. 1640
Silver and gilt brass, d. 4 ⅛ in, th. 12 ¼ in.
(d. 10.4 cm, th. 4.8 cm)

As with all carriage watches, this large-sized example strikes the hours. It has two hands: one in the middle in the form of a scepter for the alarm; the other for the hours shaped like a fleur de lis. The numerals on the dial, in openwork pierced silver, are in both Arabic and Roman. The broad banding round the case, engraved and pierced, is emblazoned with the coat-of-arms of Cardinal Richelieu. Until the end of the seventeenth century, the watch remained a luxury article that only kings, princes, and a few wealthy lords could afford. As the French court traveled to cities such as Paris, Blois, and Orleans, clockmaking workshops sprung up that soon earned a reputation to rival their German predecessors. If their timekeeping was not yet wholly reliable, such timepieces were greatly improved, both technically and artistically, by the concerted efforts of clockmakers, jewelers, and enamellers. Decoration and display often outweighed utility, as with this piece intended to be hung from a coach. We do not know if its creator belonged to the guild of clock- and watchmakers at court, which, since the reign of Henri IV, had lodged and worked out of the Bord de l'Eau gallery in the Louvre, but it is certain that Louis XIII's minister would have had recourse only to the most prestigious craftsmen and artists of the kingdom.

ANONYMOUS
The Polish Eagle of Louis XIV
Paris, mid-seventeenth century
Gold, enamel, pearls, emeralds, rubies, and garnets, 4 ⅜ in. (11.10 cm)

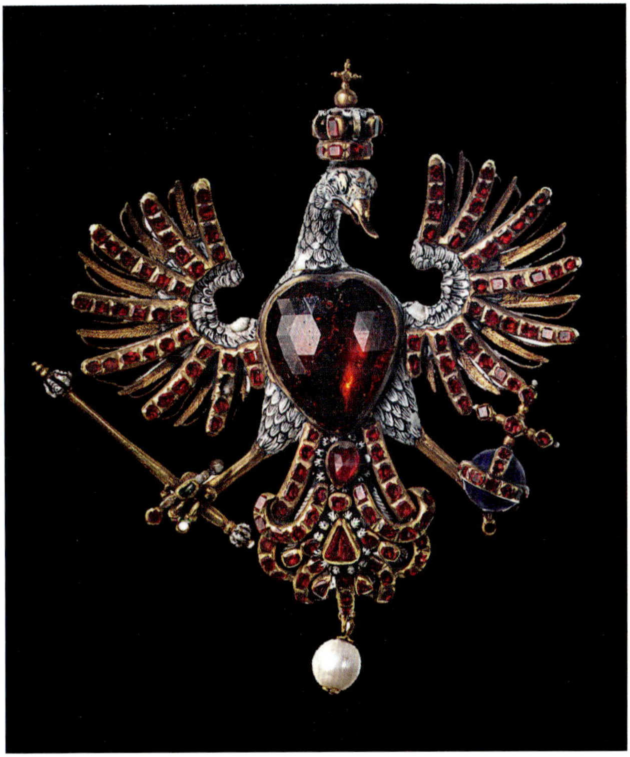

This piece, be it decoration, jewel, or insignia, is utterly exceptional for the beauty of the gems it contains, the quality of its workmanship, and because it belonged to King Louis XIV himself. Entering the royal collections prior to 1673, it formed part of the French crown jewels. Louis is believed to have ordered his goldsmith, Nicolas Pitau, to acquire this piece, once part of the estate of Louise-Marie of Gonzaga (died 1667), who had married King Ladislas IV of Poland in 1646. It represents a crowned eagle with wings outspread grasping an orb and scepter in its talons. The body of the bird is enameled and the wings and the tail are set with table-cut rubies, except for two at the level of the tail, where one is cut triangularly and the other in a heart shape. New analytical procedures have revealed that the large stone in the center—the body of the eagle—is not, as was long believed, a ruby, but a hessonite garnet. The bird represents the white eagle of Poland, symbol of the highest order of knights in the country, which was created in the fourteenth century. It was a prestigious adornment worn by the king as well by the queen, who pinned it to her bodice. Associated with the exercise of power in Ancient Rome, the eagle also appears on the blazons of the Germanic emperors and on those of Prussia and Russia. Napoleon was to adopt it as the symbol of his empire.

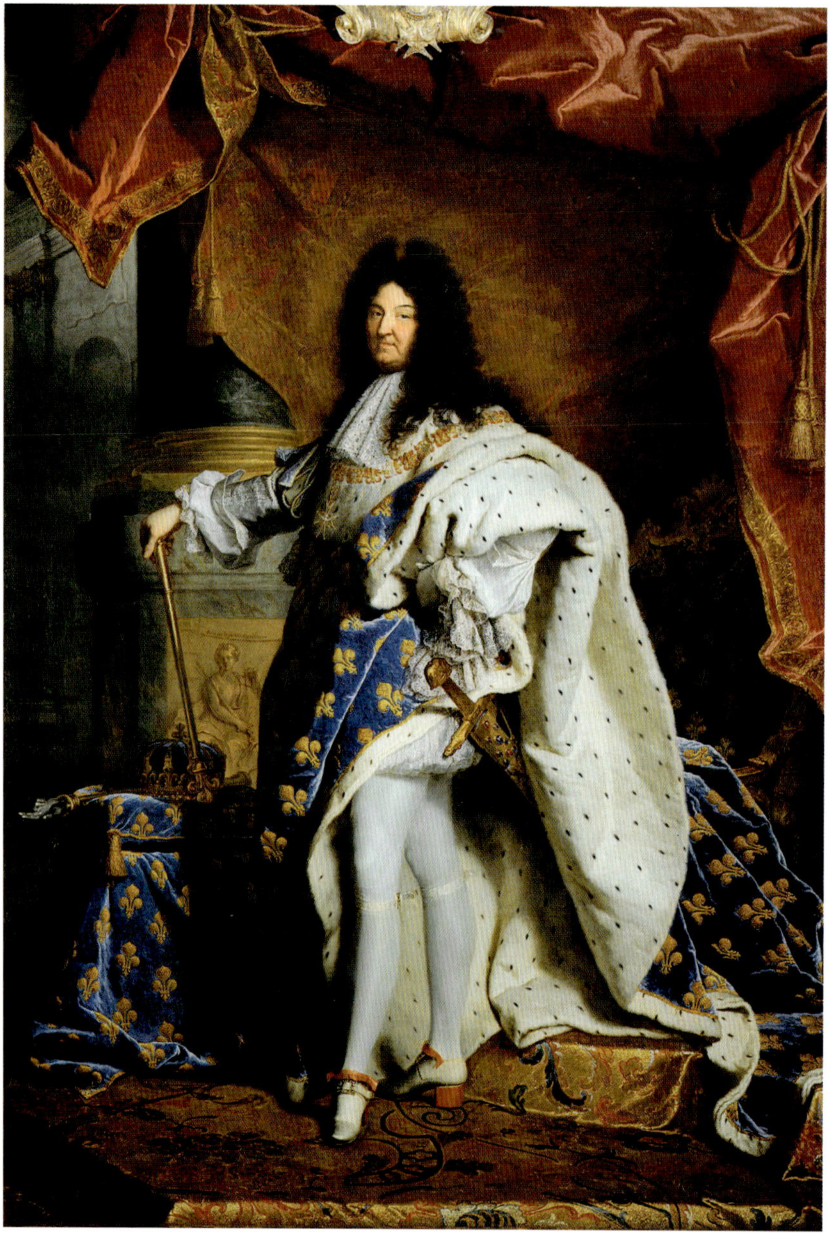

1. **HYACINTHE RIGAUD** (1659–1743)
Louis XIV (1638–1715), 1701
Oil on canvas, 9 ft. 1 in. × 6 ft. 4 ½ in. (2.77 × 1.94 m)

2. *Diamond known as the "Regent"*
1698
140.64 carats

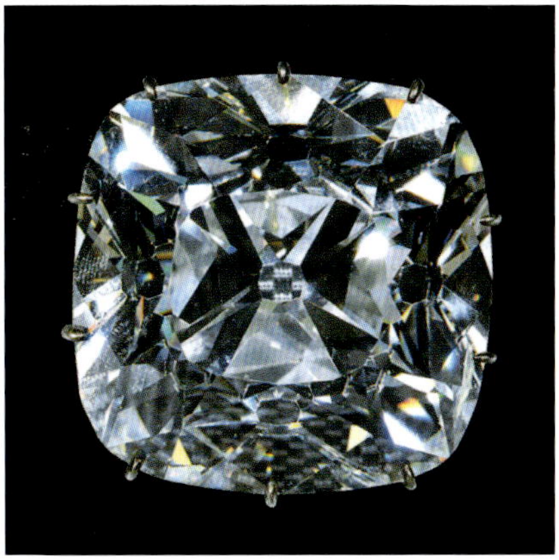

1. This portrait of the Sun King is vivid confirmation of the epithet that had already been bestowed on Louis XIV in the seventeenth century. He was sixty-three at the time this portrait was painted, and had abandoned the showy exuberance of his youth, when he appeared glittering with gems down to the buttons of his jerkin, "staggering under the weight of diamonds," as the Duc de Saint-Simon sneered in his history of Louis' court. In this ceremonial portrait, over a precious coat decorated with fleurs de lis, the king sports the chain of the Order of the Holy Spirit. His legs, sheathed in silk and adorned with garters with diamond buckles, taper off into exquisite shoes decorated with a buckle with brilliants and a bow matching the color of the heels. Swathed in red leather, these heels were Louis XIV's own invention. The right to wear red heels became a privilege and a sign of the nobility until the Revolution. On their shoes, the king and his courtiers would wear "windmill-sail" or "butterfly" bows with a buckle. It was made of gold or silver decorated with brilliants. For the less affluent, the diamond was replaced by strass. The size of the buckle swelled to the point that it encroached upon the upper part of the foot, even adopting the same shape.

2. The Regent was discovered in 1701 by a slave in the Golconda diamond mines in India, from which the majority of large diamonds come. Weighing 410 carats in its rough state, the gem was purchased by the Governor of Madras, who in 1717 sold it to the Duc d'Orléans, from whom it takes its name. Cut in London, it was reduced to 140.50 carats. Regarded as the most prestigious of all crown diamonds, the Regent was worn for the first time by Louis XV in 1721 at the reception for the Turkish ambassador and then placed in his crown for his coronation. During the Revolution, the diamond, along with many other gems was plundered. It was hidden under the eaves of a Parisian attic, until it was retrieved in 1793 and used as security against foreign debts by the Directory. It was eventually redeemed by Napoleon in 1801 and mounted by the jeweler Nitot on the guard of the consular sword the emperor wore at his anointment. It was then transferred to the crown of Charles X before moving on to Empress Eugénie's Greek-style diadem. It escaped the 1887 sale of the crown jewels and instead entered the Louvre, spending World War II concealed behind a marble mantelpiece in the château at Chambord.

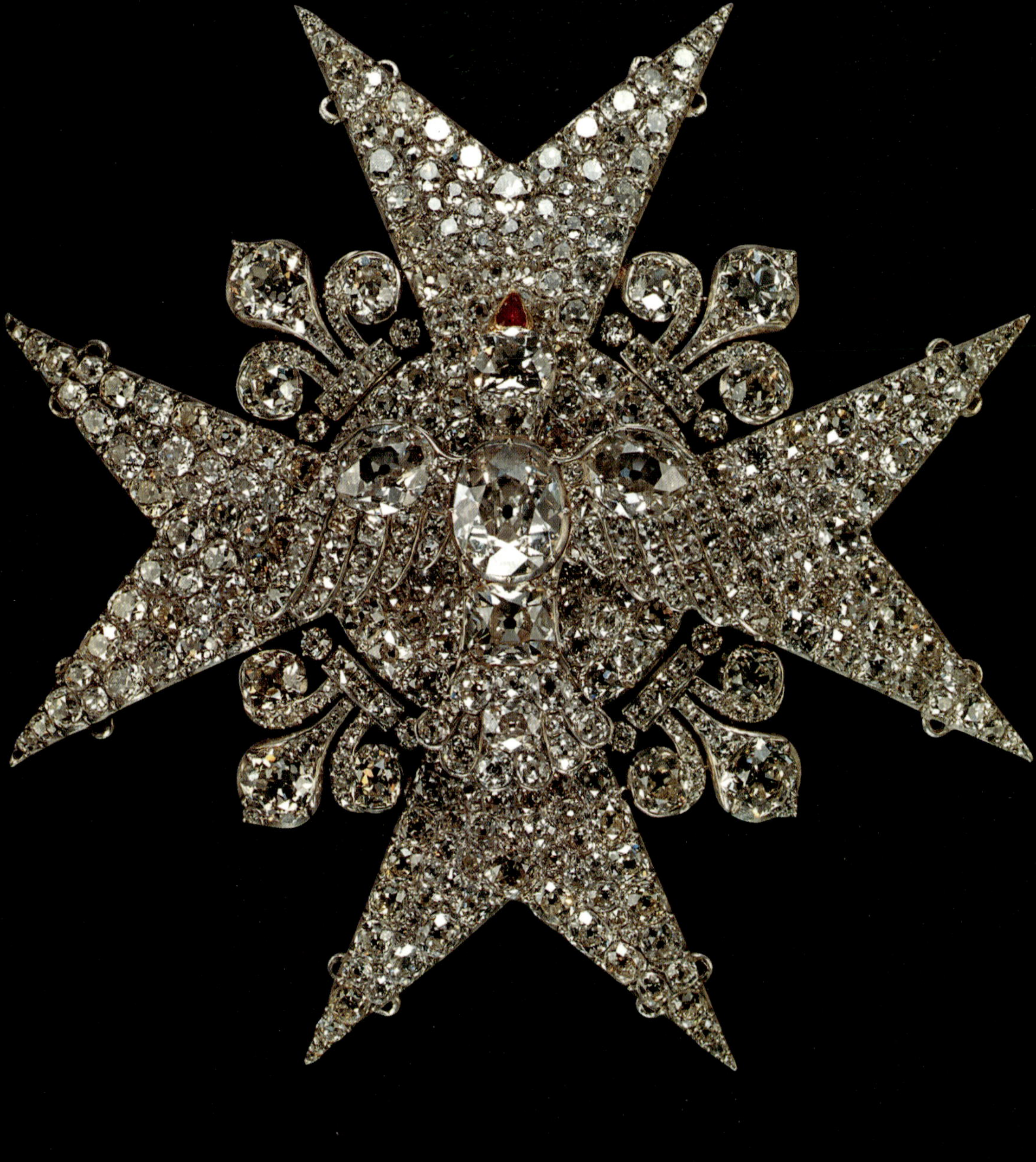

1. **ANONYMOUS**
Star of the Order of the Holy Spirit
Paris, mid-eighteenth century
Gold, silver, diamonds, and ruby, d. 4 ⅜ in. (11 cm)

2. **MAURICE-QUENTIN DE LA TOUR** (1704–1788)
Louis-Stanislas-Xavier of France, Comte de Provence,
eighteenth century
Pastel on paper, 19 ½ × 17 ¾ in. (50 × 45 cm)

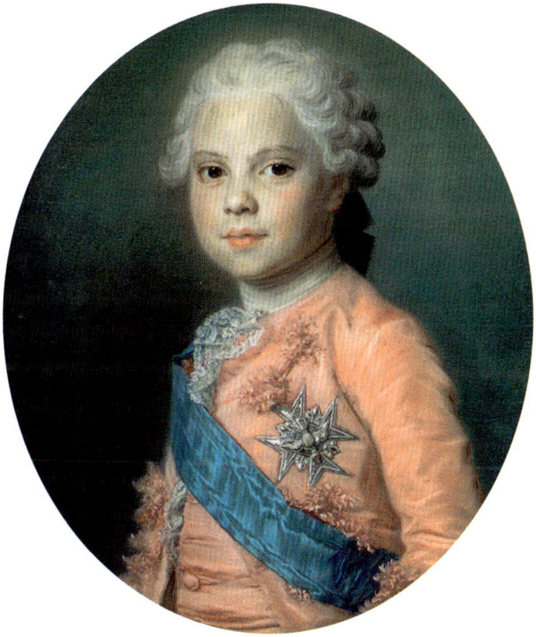

1. This decoration, composed of four hundred diamonds, was presented by Louis XV to his son-in-law or grandson—it is hard to be more specific. Both dukes of Parma became Knights of the Order of the Holy Spirit, in 1736 and in 1762 respectively. The spangled cross took as its model that of the Knights of Malta and is made of enameled gold with eight round-tipped branches. In the center is a dove with outstretched wings containing an oval diamond of 7.50 carats. Its beak is made out of a small ruby set in gold, with, at the corners, between the branches of the cross, fleurs de lis in gold, with the entire pavé set with smaller diamonds. This piece was most likely made by Jacquemin, crown jeweler from 1757 to 1773. Four rings fixed to the arms of the cross allowed it to be sewn onto the knight's vestments when it was not hung from the ribbon. On both ecclesiastical and secular crosses and pendants, the dove often symbolized the sacred (the dove of the Holy Spirit) and profane (the dove of Venus and love) simultaneously.

2. It is hard to imagine that this young stripling, Louis XVI's brother and son of the dauphin and Marie-Joseph of Saxony was to expand into the corpulent and gouty King Louis XVIII. Across his chest and passing under his arm, the boy sports the blue ribbon of the Order of the Holy Spirit, founded by Henry III in 1578. A mark of princely dignity, since the time of Henry IV the *cordon bleu* was awarded to the sons of France—those of the king, the dauphin and his eldest son—at their christening or summary baptism. They would become members of this extremely prestigious order only at their first communion, when they were given the chain made of links in the shape of the "H" of the founder (Henry III) and the fleur de lis.

CHARLES-SIMON BOUCHER, chatelaine, Paris, 1751–1752
JACQUES-JÉRÔME GUDIN, watch, Paris, 1750–1751
Round watch with matching chatelaine
Gold, gilt brass, enamel, diamond, and agate, d. 1 ¾ in., th. 1 in.
(d. 4.80 cm, th. 2.60 cm)

This ravishing jewel is composed of two independent elements: a chatelaine and a watch. The chatelaine is attached to the belt by an elaborate hook, here composed of several jointed elements. The winding key for the watch and an agate seal are suspended at the end of two small chains. One face of the watch takes the form of a white enamel case—missing the hands—while the other is decorated. The delicate roses painted on the guilloched ground and the refined blend of colors in translucent green enamel and gold suggests that this piece was intended to be worn by a woman, a theory confirmed by the inscription "*Léonora*" in Gothic script on the seal. Chatelaine and watch sets were the height of fashion for both men and women in the second half of the eighteenth century, and this example displays all the grace and harmony of the Louis XV style. Perhaps it was a love token. After all, the Enlightenment was not only the Age of Reason, it was also the time of the Man of Feeling, and a vast cohort of boxes, rings, and seals were engraved with rebuses concealing declarations of love. Hidden from prying eyes, the presence of her Christian name reminds the lady that this jewel was given to her and that she is loved.

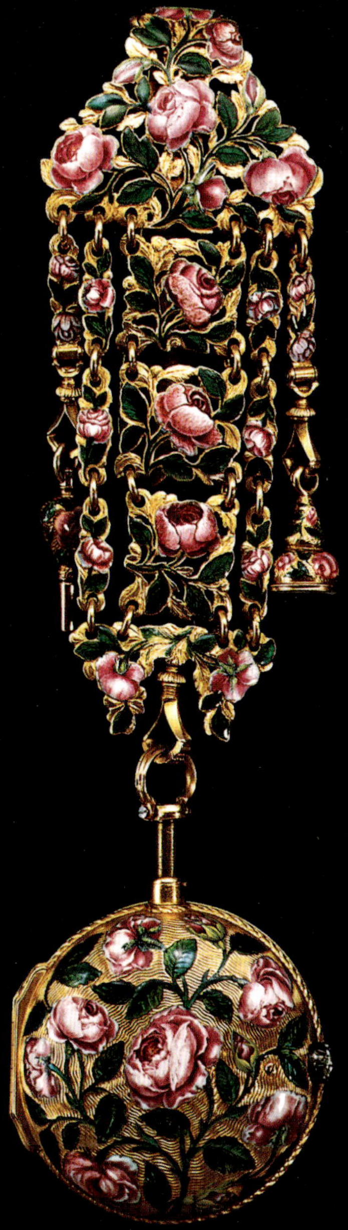

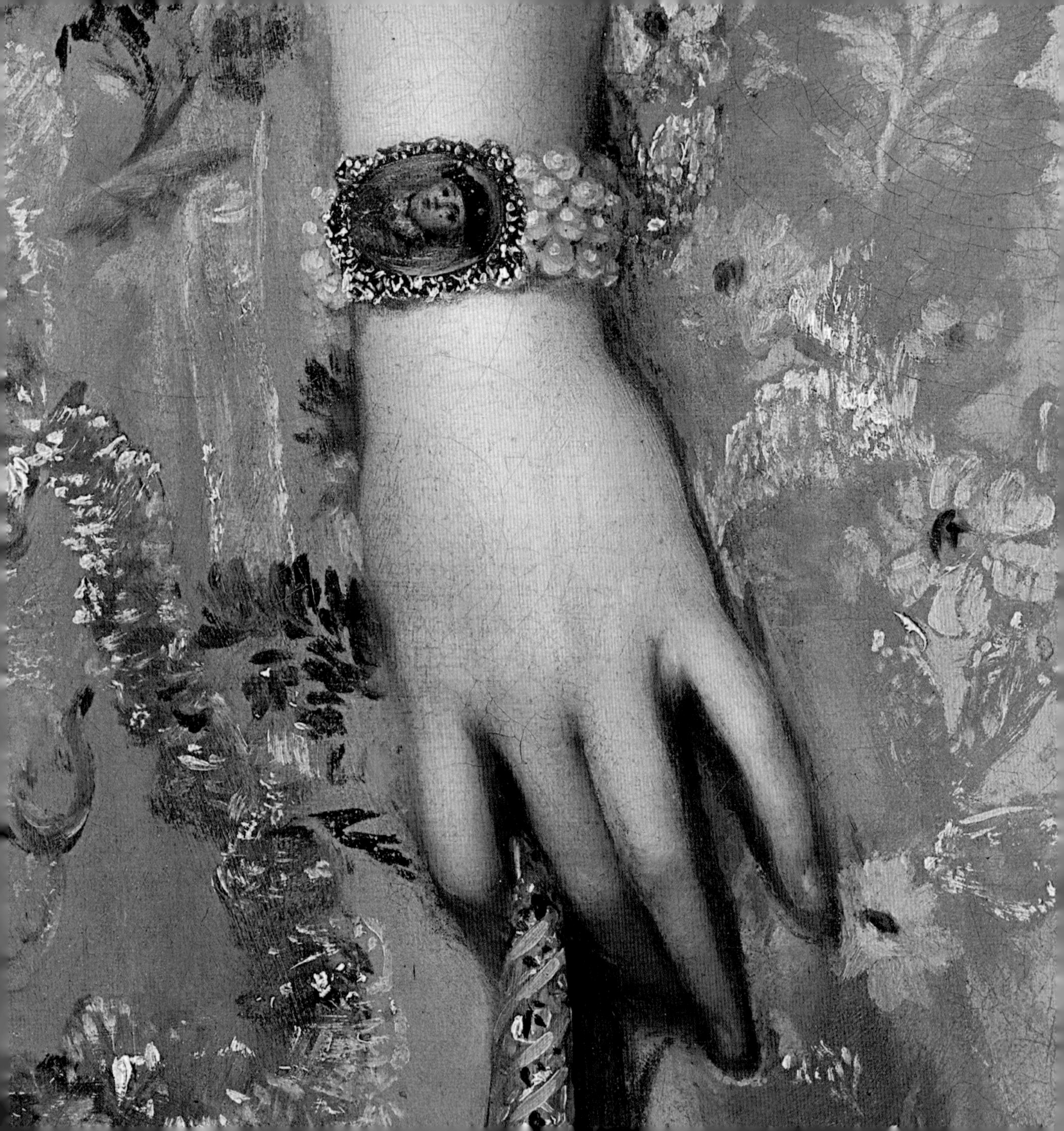

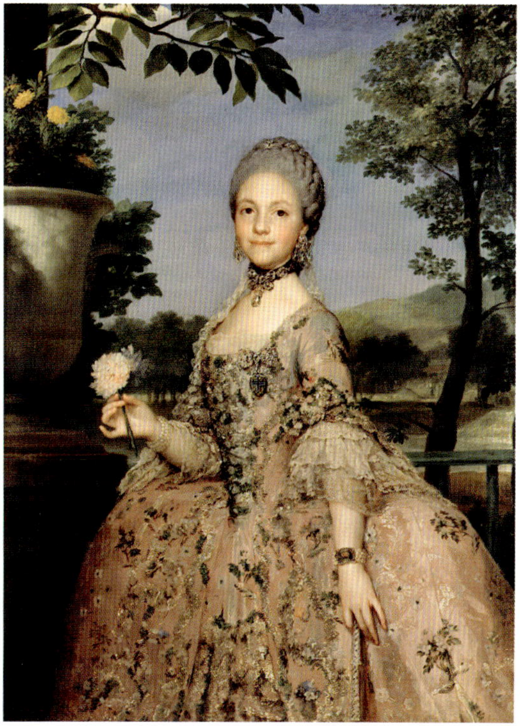

ANTON-RAPHAEL MENGS (1728–1779)
Maria-Luisa of Parma,
Princess of the Asturias, 1765
Oil on canvas, 4 ft. 2 ¾ in. × 3 ft. 2 in (129 × 97 cm)

Maria-Luisa of Parma, granddaughter of Louis XIV, was only fourteen years old when she married her cousin Charles IV of Spain, then aged seventeen, in 1765. The event is commemorated in this portrait, which is infinitely more flattering than that of Charles IV and his family painted by Goya in 1800. It represents a very beautiful and carefree young woman (blissfully unaware that she will give birth to fifteen children) holding a spray of pinks, the symbol of love. Such gorgeous apparel is a superb example of the refined ostentation characteristic of eighteenth-century European courts. Several jewels set with diamonds trim the gorgeous embroidered gown inspired by French styles, and are undoubtedly the work of the Parisian jewelers invited to the Spanish court. A bow, similarly dusted with diamonds, and which could equally be used to decorate her bodice, covers the black velvet choker (or *carcanet*) snug about her neck. In about 1700, the development of a new diamond cut allowed gems to be displayed to even better effect. Both the *girandole* earrings (ear pendants with three drops) and the bejeweled bow derive from pattern-book engravings, an inexhaustible source of new designs. The diamond knot at the base of Maria-Luisa's low neckline is fastened with a spangled cross decoration (known as a *cruz estrellada*), an indicator of social status, since, apart from sovereigns, it was an insignia only a handful of high-ranking individuals were permitted to wear. Finally, the queen's wrists are embellished with two bracelets of several rows of pearls with, in the center, a miniature that one can only imagine to be a portrait of her husband.

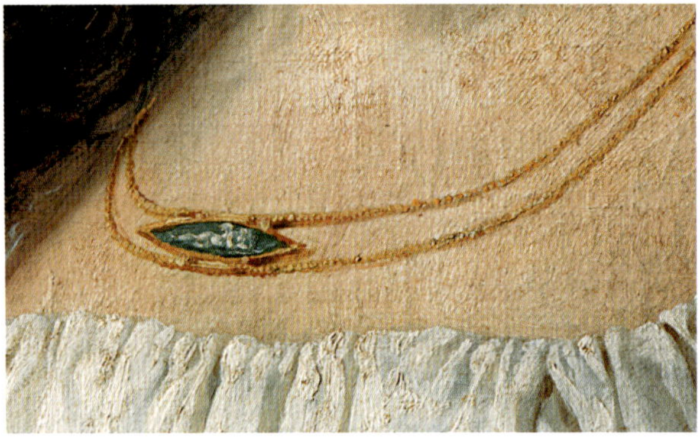

ANTOINE-JEAN GROS (1771–1835)
Madame Pasteur, 1795–1796
Oil on canvas, 34 ¼ × 26 ⅜ in. (87 × 67 cm)

The young woman depicted by the painter Gros in 1795 takes us back to the stormy period of the Directory (1795–99) through which, following the bloody years of the French Revolutionary Terror, a wind of freedom was blowing. It was an unbuttoned period, dominated by the so-called Merveilleuses, the first women to dress *à la grecque*, i.e. in provocatively light muslin dresses. This scandalous get-up, whose top left little to the imagination and whose fine fabrics exposed the legs to public scrutiny, had been launched by the most famous of these extravagant creatures, Madame Tallien. "Bracelets, rings adorned what was otherwise near total nudity, her Antique sandals were tied with cords of gold and silk and fastened by a precious jewel," an observer noted.

The young woman shown here is altogether more modest. Painted in Genoa while General Bonaparte was in Italy, Madame Pasteur belonged to a family of bankers originally from the Jura. Arms crossed, she wears a simple muslin dress and only her curly hairstyle (powdered periwigs having been consigned to oblivion) and somewhat understated jewelry hint that she is indeed a follower of fashion. Braided above the ears into tresses known as *cadenettes*, her hair is stuck with two large arrow-shaped pins and her throat adorned with a double gold chain bearing a diamond-shaped enameled medallion representing a cupid brandishing his bow. It is a light necklet with two slender *jaseron* chains redolent of the so-called *esclavage* ("slavery") chain, usually formed of three medallions, which would become more widespread during the Empire period of 1804–15, and even reach the countryside where it became a wedding token.

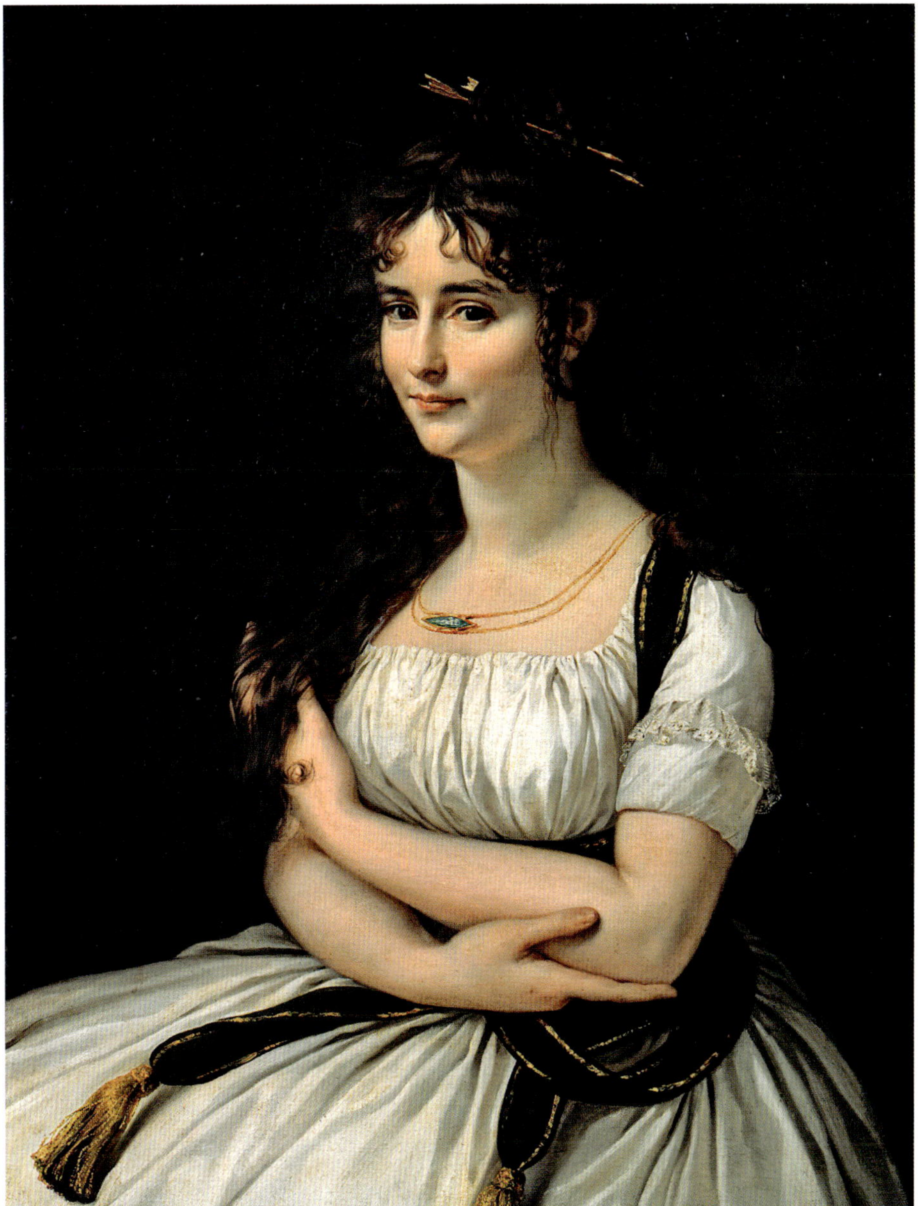

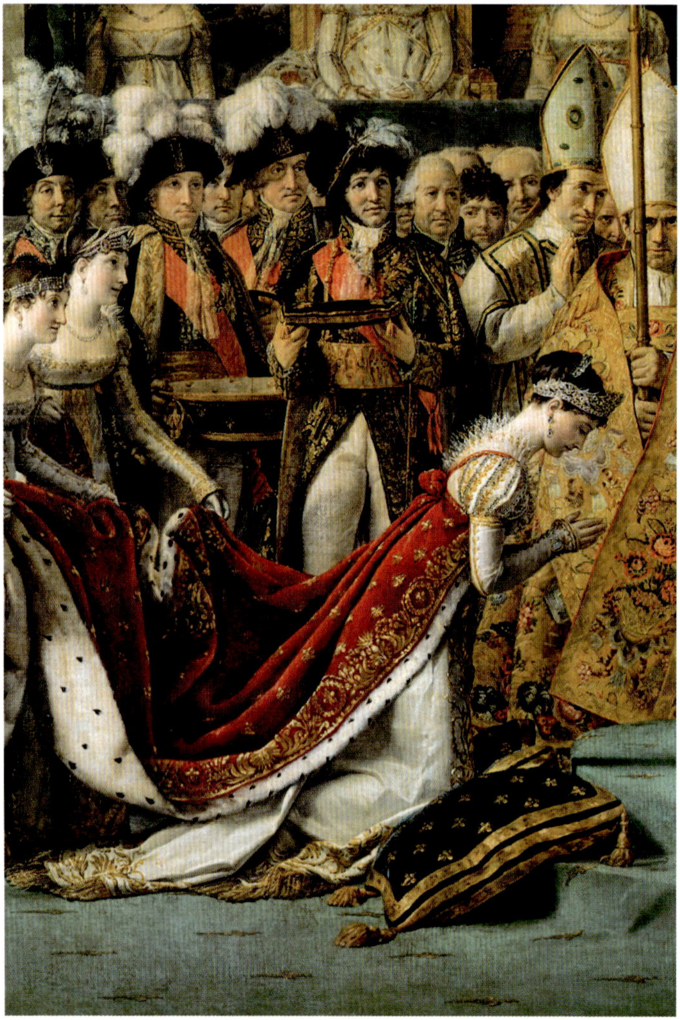

JACQUES-LOUIS DAVID (1748–1825)
The Coronation of the Emperor and Empress (the Consecration), 1805–1807
Oil on canvas, 20 ft 7 ½ in. × 32 ft. 1 in. (6.29 × 9.79 m)

The ceremony of the consecration of Napoleon I on December 2, 1804, was the object of meticulous preparations concerning protocol and appearance. Josephine was six years older than her imperial husband, and she had to appear in the requisite splendor and elegance befitting such an occasion. Wearing make up by the painter Jean-Baptiste Isabey and draped in a vast red velvet coat strewn with imperial bees and lined in ermine, Josephine was at the pinnacle of her beauty. Presented in profile by the painter just as she receives the crown from the hands of Napoleon, the empress's hair is dressed with a diamond diadem-comb. Her forehead is girded by a diadem of rosettes and florets swathed in more than a thousand diamonds (it is now in a private collection in New York), while her wrists are adorned with two cameo bracelets.

It is doubtful that the jewelry depicted by David is entirely accurate; the painter executed this painting on Napoleon's orders a full year after the coronation. Although the crown and belt of Josephine's robe were real enough and made by the court jeweler, Marguerite, with diamonds from the crown collection, the diadem does not seem to match the piece featured at the coronation, which was made of emeralds or amethysts and diamonds, with matching necklace and earrings that have since vanished. In any event, the princesses and ladies attending the ceremony boasted a dazzling array of diamond diadems or headbands; those of Madame de Valette and Queen Hortense, in the shape of an ear of wheat, were to serve as models for the crowning of Queen Victoria.

PIERRE-LOUIS BOUVIER (1765–1836)
Portrait of Empress Josephine, 1812
Miniature on ivory, d. 3 ⅝ in. (9.3 cm)

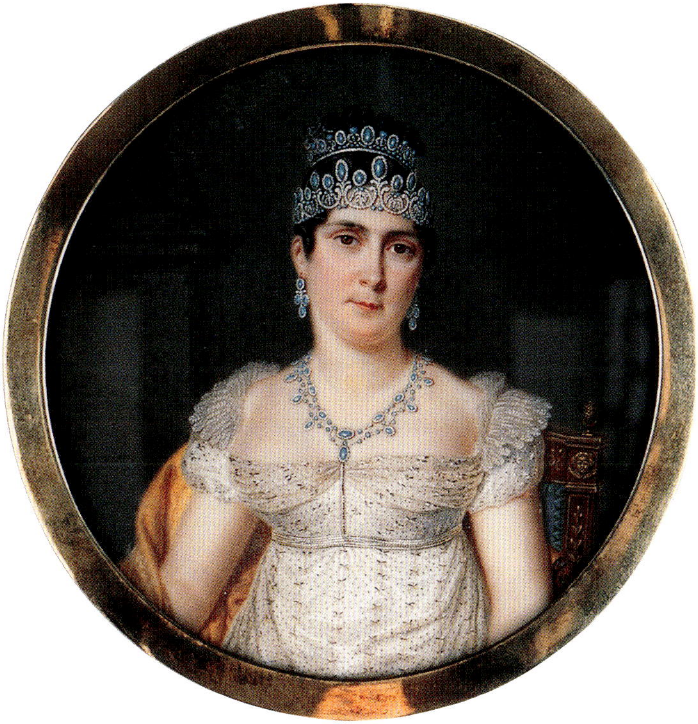

Empress Josephine, wife of Napoleon I, has gone down in history for her considerable allure and her propensity to spend money like water—in the same way Queen Marie-Antoinette had done a few years previously. Careless of debts that Napoleon always ended up settling, Josephine had an insatiable appetite for clothes and jewels, matching the color of her attire with that of the drawing-room in which she received visitors, and the color of her jewelry with that of her garments.

The last inventory of the empress's property, drawn up posthumously in 1814, features an impressive list of her decorative items, in one hundred lots of jewels, including pearls and precious stones waiting to be mounted onto rings, bracelets, and brooches. The roll call is astonishing: cameos, rubies, opals, emeralds, agates, petrified wood, malachite, mosaic, brilliants, steel, jet.... Such gemstones and bizarre materials were used in the manufacture of her parures, jewelry ensembles that had already existed in the previous century but which in the Empire were taking on new forms. Each set consisted of a diadem-comb, a necklace, two bracelets, and pendant earrings, often complemented by a headband, belt clasps and sleeve-buttons. Josephine's coffers and jewel-cases also overflowed with parures in semi-precious stones, such as amethysts, coral, cornelian and turquoise, whose various hues were more in keeping with morning or outdoor wear.

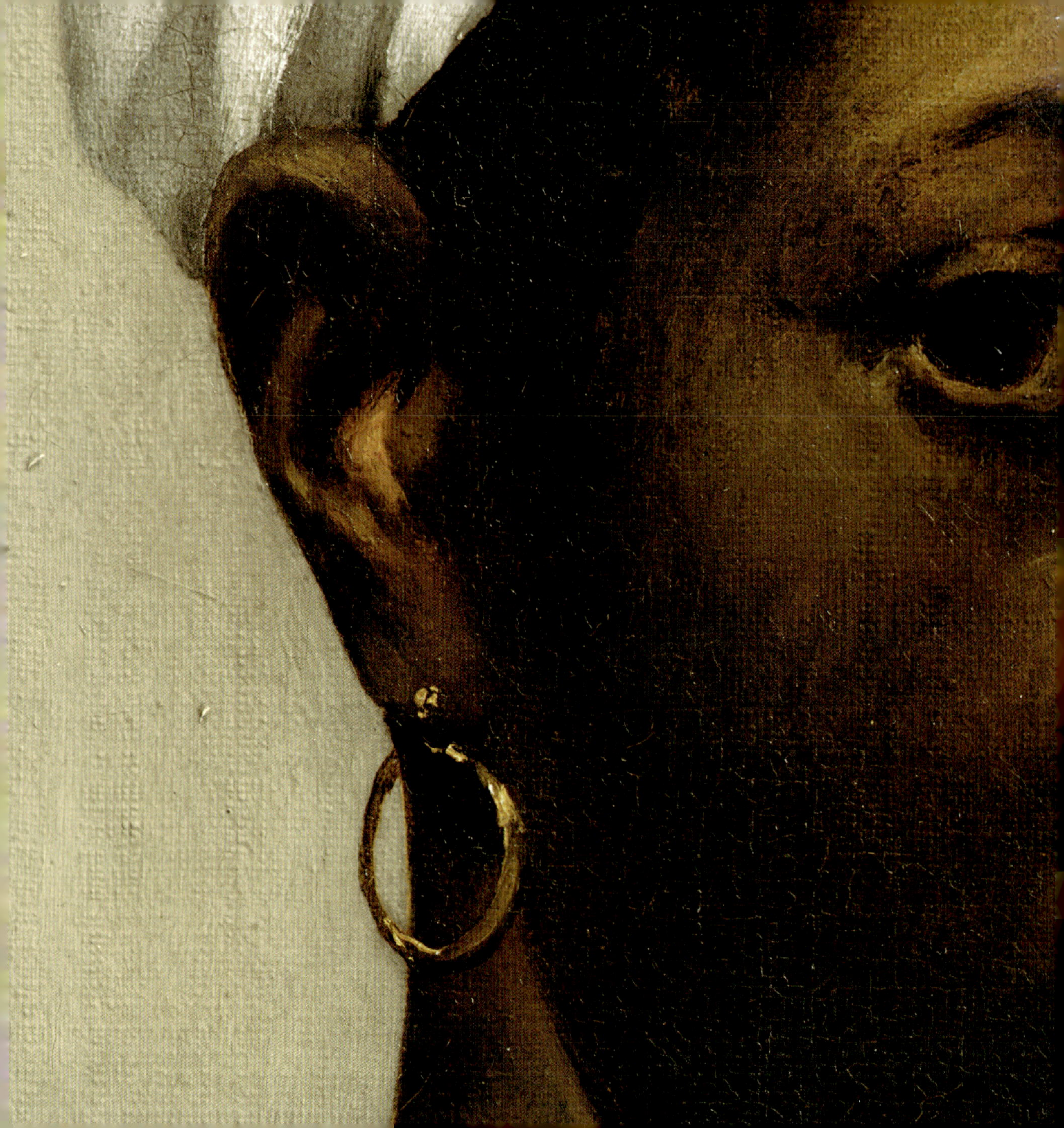

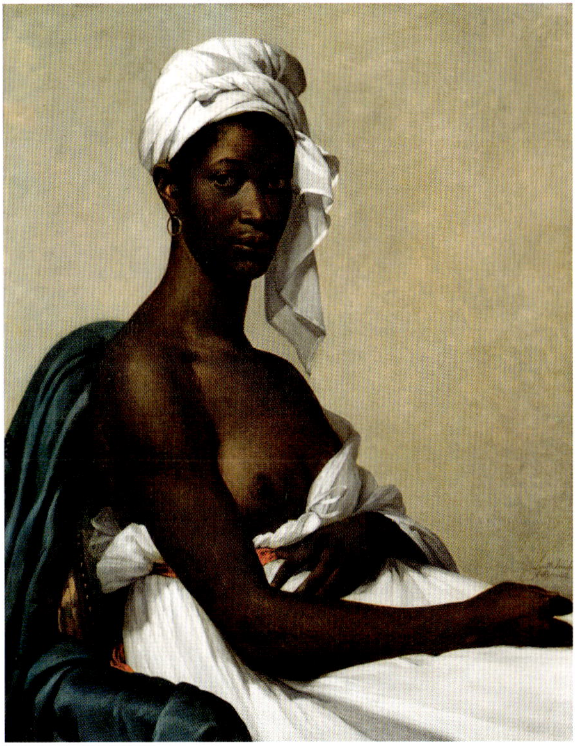

MARIE-GUILLEMINE BENOIST (1768–1826)
Portrait of a Black Woman, Salon of 1800
Oil on canvas, 31 ⅞ × 25 ½ in. (81 × 65 cm)

This picture is believed to depict a servant—a slave, in all probability—brought back from the French West Indies by the artist's brother-in-law. At the time, the artist was certainly courting scandal by representing a semi-nude black model in a classical pose at the official Salon. Criticism was not long in coming and reflected the inherent racism of the time: "So ghastly [and] it's a pretty white hand that has presented us with all this blackness!"

The model's ebony-black skin is set off by her snow-white chemise and draped turban. The white and black are punctuated only by a single gold earring. This type of ring had a complex origin and a long history: worn by men as much as women, except during the Renaissance it was for long a symbol of submission or transgression. Originating, like the *robe-chemise* or shirtwaist, in the French Antilles, these rings were known as *créoles* at the end of the eighteenth century and soon became a fad. Several young women of the court painted by Vigée-Lebrun sport just such *créoles* bedecked in pearls. During the Revolution and the Directory period, although still made of gold, the rings became less showy and were increasingly a male accessory. In iconography, however, the African origin of these *créoles* prevailed, and they appeared on depictions of the Magi or on black servants—as this portrait confirms.

FRANÇOIS-REGNAULT NITOT (1779–1853)
Parure of the Empress Marie-Louise, Paris, 1810
Gold and glass micro-mosaic, necklace: 17 ¾ in. (45 cm); bracelets: 7 ¼ in. (18.5 cm); comb: 4 ⅜ in. (11 cm); earrings: 1 ¾ in. (4.3 cm)

It only goes to show that one can be an empress and display dazzling diamonds at official functions, and yet also yield to the temptations of less conventional fashions. Among the innumerable sets of jewels Marie-Louise received from Napoleon in April 1810 as wedding presents was this relatively modest if extremely delicate piece, made from micro-mosaic. Like the cameo, this novelty was all the rage during the Empire period. Italian, or more precisely Roman artists, schooled in the techniques of mosaic since antiquity, had become past masters in the art of assembling tiny particles of colored glass (*tesserae*) into flowers, landscapes, or other scenes, which were then made into furniture, pictures, or jewels. Comprising no less than ten medallions, this parure was clearly crafted in Italy. It consists of a necklace, a comb, two bracelets, and two pendant earrings illustrated with Roman ruins. The subjects are framed in blue *pâte de verre*.

The mount, on the other hand, was entrusted to François-Regnault Nitot, official jeweler to the court, who set off the medallions with a succession of vine-leaves and bunches of grapes minutely engraved in gold. The whole set was part of the crown treasure carried off by Marie-Louise to Austria on the fall of the Empire in 1814, and were returned to France by Emperor Francis II. During the Second Empire (1852–70), it was probably Empress Eugénie who ordered the jewel-case in red shagreen, in which the ensemble is still preserved and on which are inscribed the words: "Diamonds of the Crown; Parure in gold and mosaic." Purchased in 1887 by a private individual, the pieces were eventually acquired by the Société des Amis du Louvre over a century later in 2001.

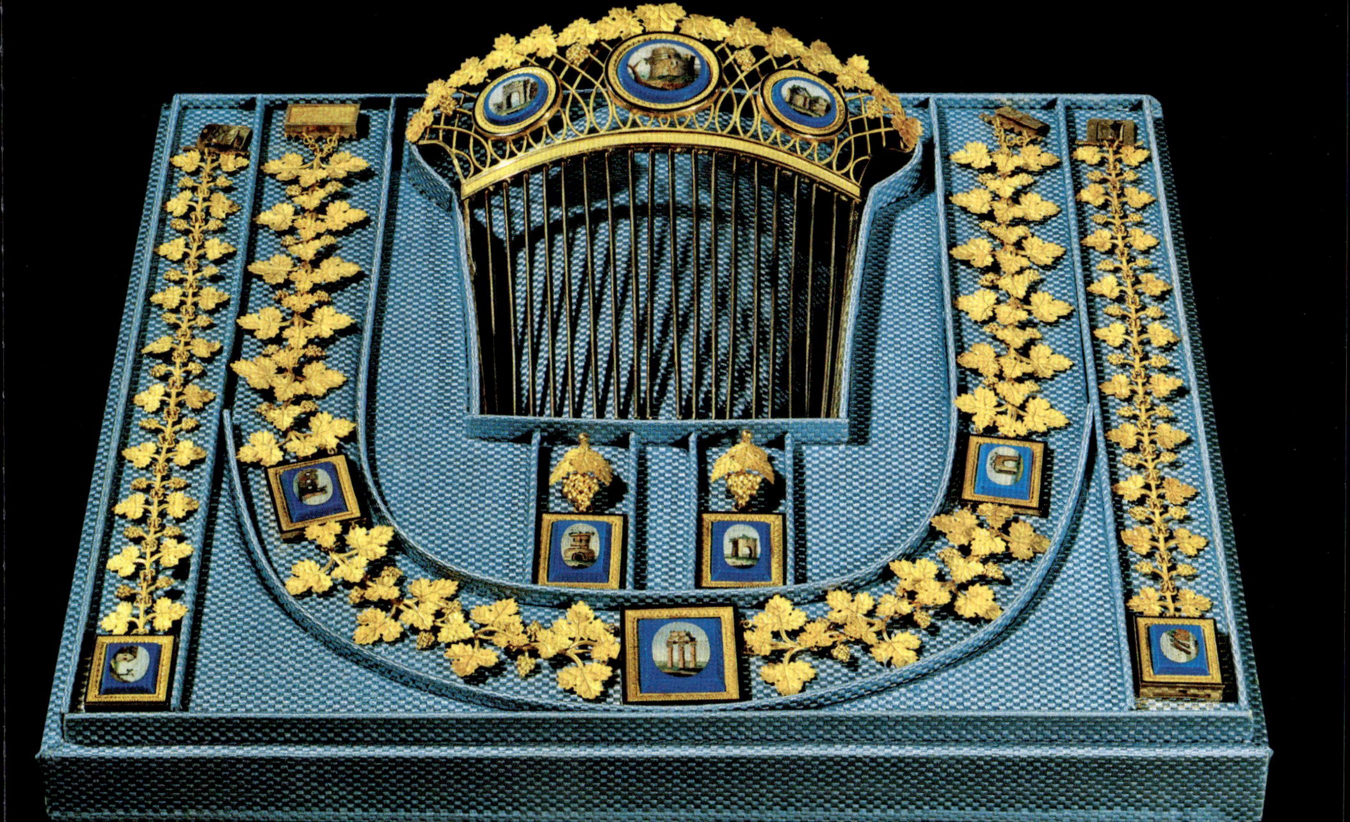

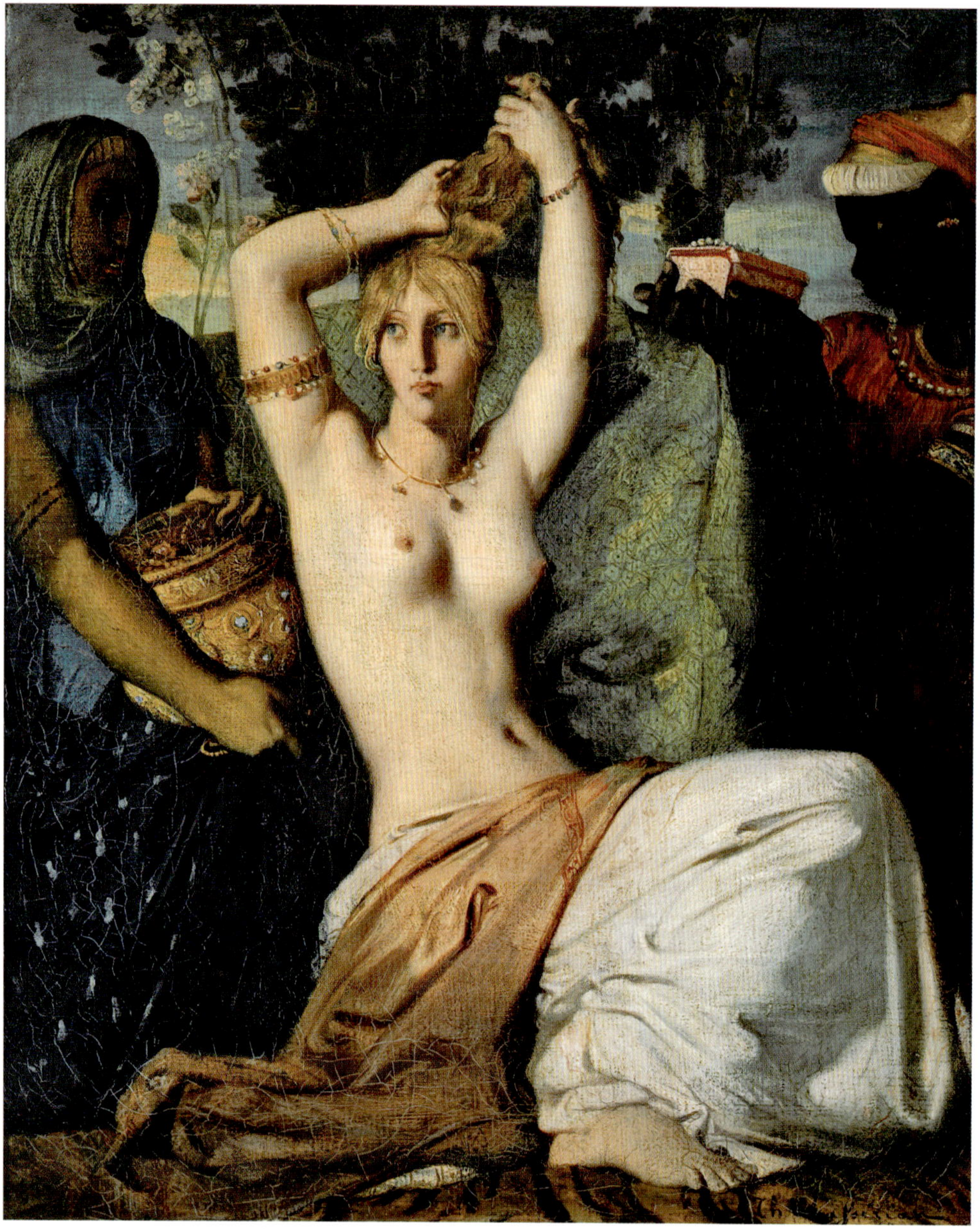

1. **THÉODORE CHASSÉRIAU** (1819–1856)
The Toilet of Esther or *Esther Preparing herself to Meet King Assuerus*, 1841
Oil on canvas, 18 × 14 in. (45.5 × 35.5 cm)

2. **ANONYMOUS**
Necklace
Cerveteri, 480–460 BCE
Gold, filigree, and stamping, 1 ¼ × 8 ½ in. (3.3 × 21.4 cm)

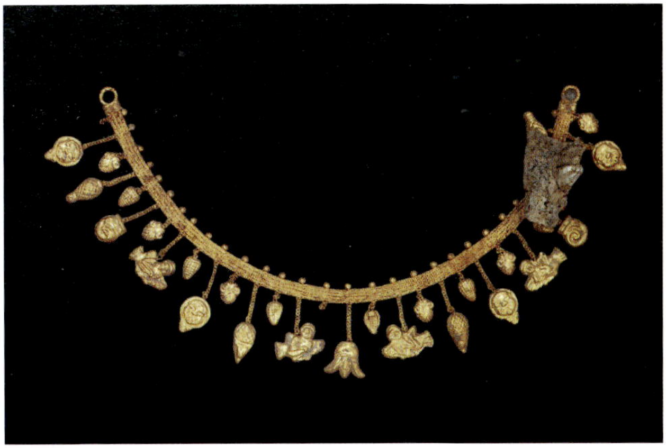

1. For this painting, Chassériau, a painter familiar with biblical and classical subjects, turned to the Book of Esther from the Old Testament, which features the beautiful Jewish woman chosen as the wife of Assuerus, the all-powerful king of the Persians. The painter depicts Esther as she leaves her bath and prepares for her introduction to the king: "Her body was now soft like the lotus petal and smelt of roses, jasmine, and myrrh." Chassériau traveled to Algeria five years after he painted this work, yet he evokes a nineteenth-century impression of the Orient through the sensual figure of the young woman. She gracefully lifts her hair in a gesture that exposes to advantage arms laden with four bracelets of gold and precious stones. She wears a gold necklace with pearls and pendants redolent of the antique-style jewels favored around 1840, and one imagines that the eunuch Hegai and the maidservant standing near, themselves dressed in gold, will fetch other jewels from the exquisite caskets nearby. The artist returns to the familiar theme of the woman at her toilet, but adds elements of the sensuality of Ingres's odalisques, which Théophile Gautier captured so well in the following lines from his verse collection *Émaux et Camées*: "Slipping from shoulder to hip/, The nonchalantly folded chemise/Like a white turtle-dove/ Dropped forsaken at her white feet."

2. In the nineteenth century the vast array of forms and delicacy of technique offered by Greek and Roman jewelry gave rise to copies and pastiches almost as entrancing as the originals. This particular Etruscan necklace belonged to the collection of Marquis Campana (1807–1880), a major collector of Etruscan and Italic jewels, from whom Napoleon III purchased it in 1861. It consists of a flat-mesh gold-filigree braid in twisted wire, with stamped gold pendants suspended from fine chains in the form of palmettes, pine-cones, sirens, Gorgon masks, lotus flowers, and spirals. Less poetically, attached to the necklace, which was unearthed in a tomb close to the remains of a young girl, there hangs a fragment of jaw complete with tooth.

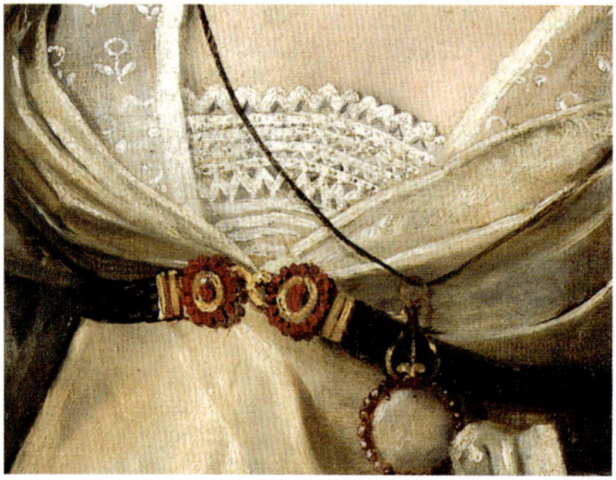

FRENCH SCHOOL
The Three Ladies of Ghent, 1816–1817
Oil on canvas, 4 ft. 4 in. × 3 ft. 5 in. (1.32 × 1.05 m)

Since fashions invariably change, artists often prefer to emphasize the psychological aspect of their models, referring only sketchily to their attire, as with the painter David, for instance. This triple portrait, on the other hand, showing Madame Morel de Tangry, the wife of an alderman of Courtrai, with two of her daughters, is a veritable catalogue of late Empire costume and accessories. All three women, who could be taken to symbolize the three ages of life—youth, maturity, and old age—look rather alike, but their differences are highlighted by a garment and a jewel.

Secured by two buckles, the belt around the dress of the woman standing to the left appears to be made of hair. Since the eighteenth century, craftsmen had used locks of hair to make ingenuous pieces of sentimental jewelry, gifts, or souvenirs of separation or bereavement. This fashion gained ground, as did the expertise of the artists, who proceeded to braid hair into bracelets, chains, and even long rope-style necklaces (known as *sautoirs*), watch-chains, and belts. The long chains draped over the bodice of Madame Morel de Tangry, seated, and of her daughter, on the other hand, are made of gold. This was a more traditional adornment, as is the coral necklace with several rows of pearls, which came back into vogue during the Empire period with the exploitation of Mediterranean coral. Another accessory-cum-jewel marked this period—the comb, visible in the hair of the young lady on the right. The decorated part is a band that could be changed to suit. Adorned with turquoise, amethyst, or coral, it would be chosen to complement the shade of the gown.

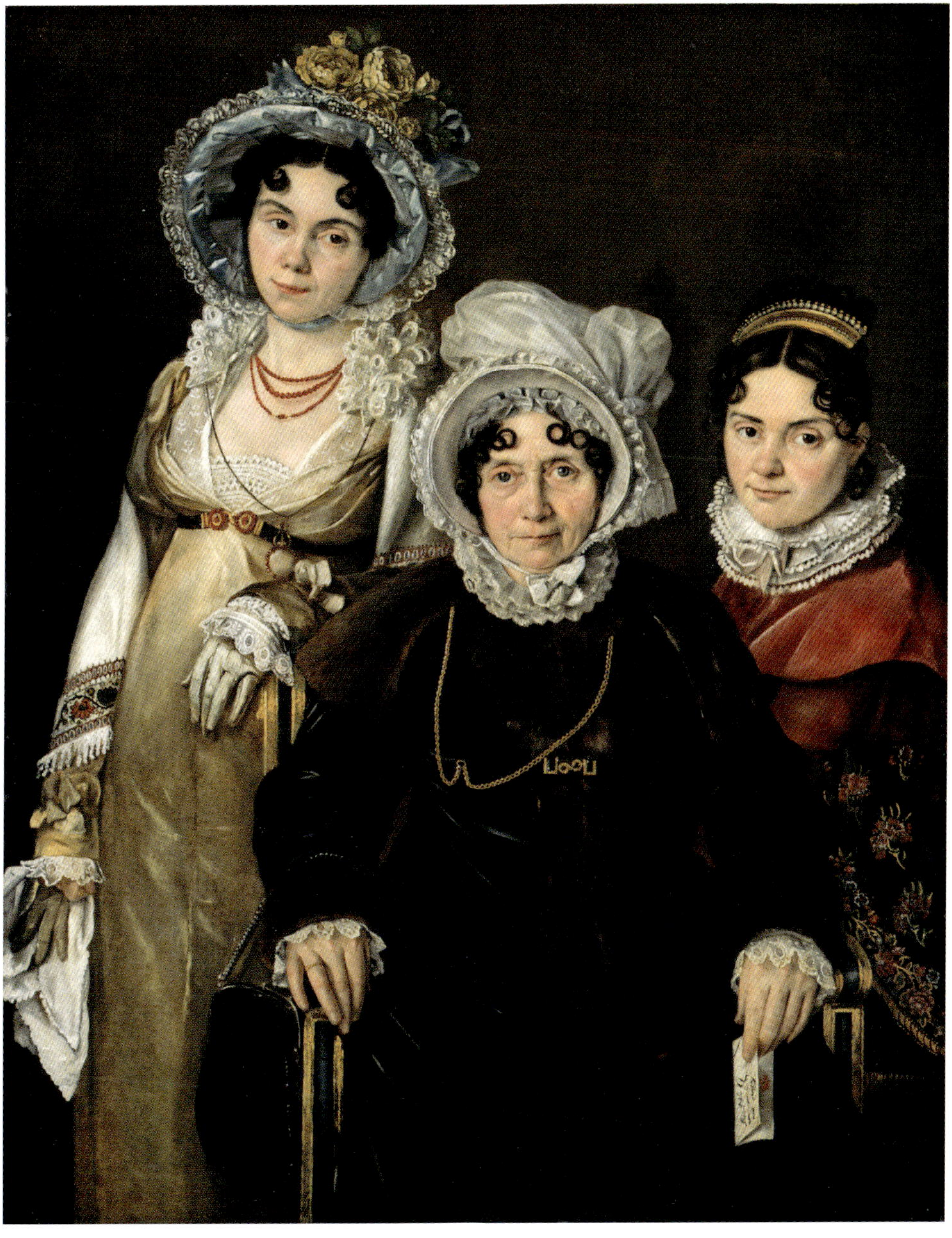

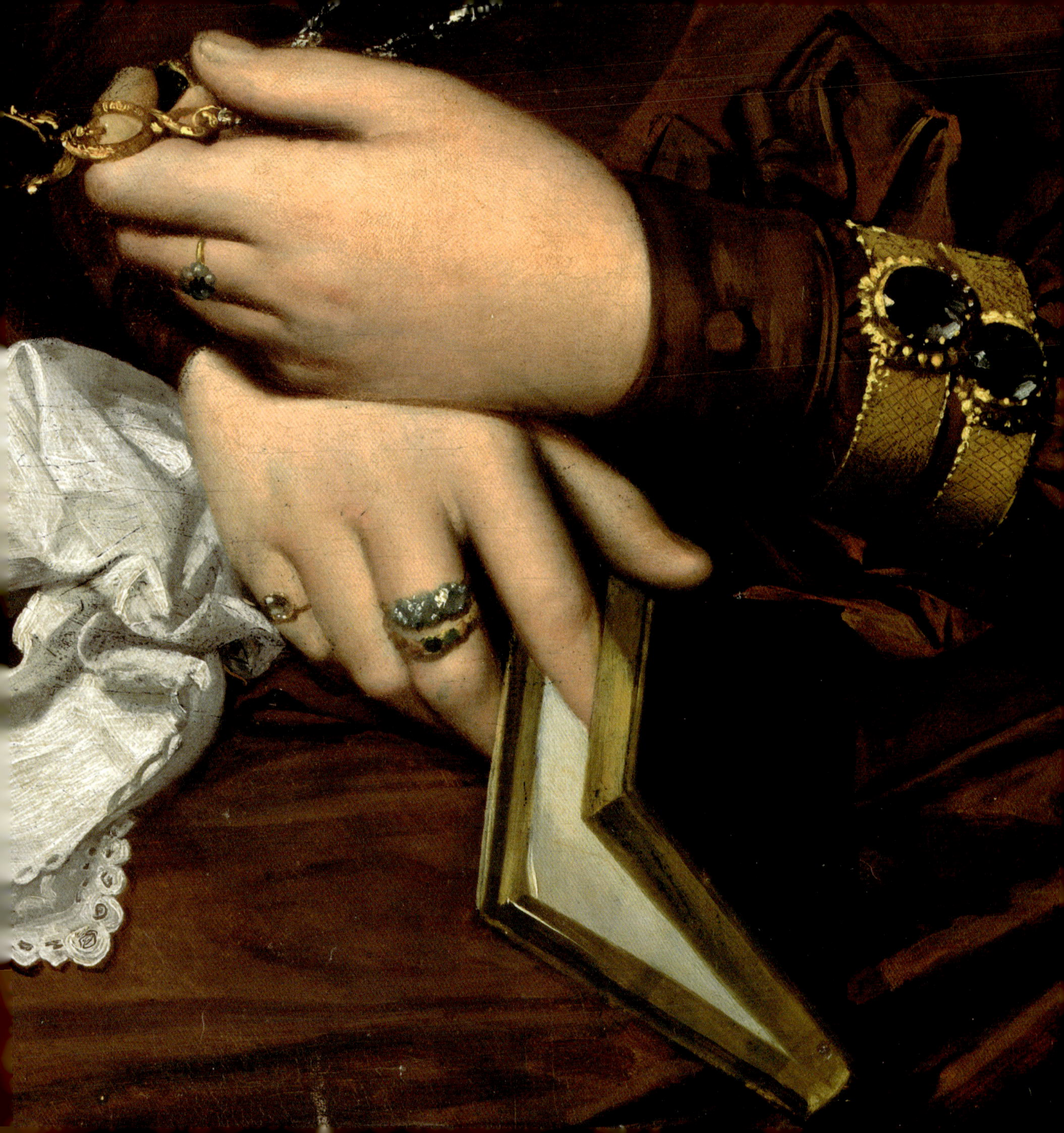

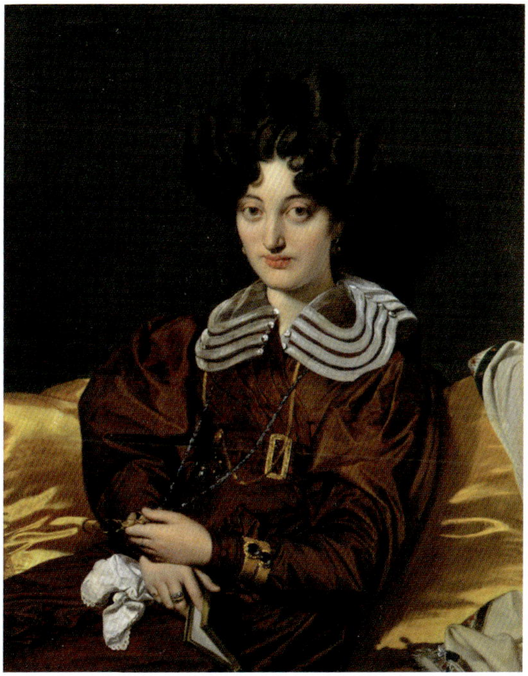

JEAN-AUGUSTE-DOMINIQUE INGRES
(1780–1867)
Madame Marcotte, 1826
Oil on canvas, 36 ½ × 29 in. (93 × 74 cm)

If art historians regard Ingres as the preeminent painter of women, for historians of costume his portraits are an inexhaustible resource for the study of fashions between the First and Second Empires. The artist's attention to the tiniest detail of dress allows the historian to pinpoint developments in taste and provides invaluable information about how, for instance, shawls were draped, hair was styled, or jewelry shown to its best advantage. This portrait is full of such lessons. Married to a treasury secretary, Marie Marcotte was twenty-three when she sat for Ingres, a friend of her brother-in-law. Breathtakingly pretty she is not. Crowned by an egg-shaped hairstyle *en coques*, her face is the epitome of boredom, but her dress bristles with telling details. The organdie neckline adds a note of white to the shimmering, russet-coloured silk gown around which runs a broad belt secured by a buckle. The long, gold *sautoir* to which the lorgnette is fixed partly conceals the chatelaine attached to the belt. This accessory, which had disappeared since the eighteenth century with the loose-fitting gowns of the Empire, reappeared during the Bourbon Restoration of 1814–30 when waists came back into fashion. Instead of wearing one broad bracelet on each wrist, Madame Marcotte chose to sport two on the same arm. How they were made is clear enough: the strap is a gold weave of braided mesh, while the mount for the amethysts is dusted in *grenetis*. Jewelry was at the time undergoing a revival. The Etruscan *grenetis* or gold-dust technique, in which particles of the metal are fused into a single body, had been recently rediscovered, while woven mesh, forgotten since the Renaissance, was widely employed again around 1830.

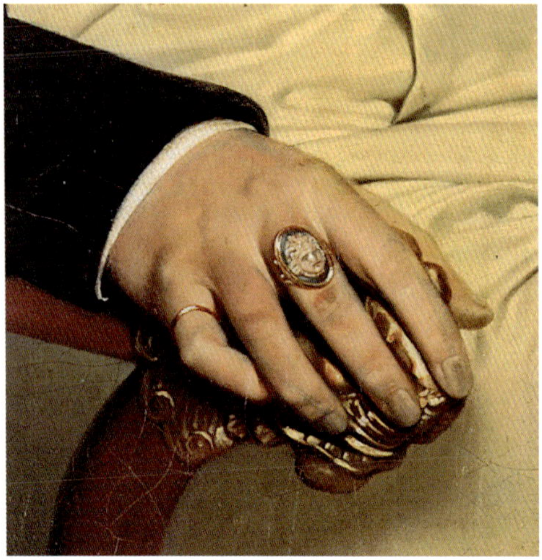

JEAN-AUGUSTE-DOMINIQUE INGRES (1780–1867)
Monsieur Rivière, 1804
Oil on canvas, 3 ft. 9 ¼ in. × 35 ½ in. (115 × 90 cm)

This picture is the last in a trilogy featuring the members of the Rivière family: father, mother, and daughter. Although each is treated differently, the social standing of each sitter is much emphasized. The Rivières were nothing if not bourgeois, proud of their success, but not showy. Monsieur Rivière, son of a family of administrators who had served the king during the Ancien Régime, was forty-four years old when he asked the young Ingres, who had recently carried off the much-vaunted Prix de Rome, to paint him and his family. A fine, engaging-looking man, and a well-off collector and lover of art, Rivière has taken up a relaxed pose, with legs crossed and his left hand in his waistcoat. Dressed casually in coat and fitted breeches, he presents no outward signs of wealth: no gold tie-pin, no decorations on his clothing, and no clunking knick-knacks swinging at the belt, all of which were customary male adornments at the time. Rivière shows no more than a carnelian watch-key that peeks out of the waistcoat and hints at the chain and timepiece in the fob-pocket. Watch keys, which remained in use until the invention of the winder in about 1850, were then pieces of authentic jewelry carved from hardstone and sometimes engraved with a rebus, and displayed in full view. The hand draped over the arm of the chair boasts two rings, the most conspicuous decorated with a cameo or intaglio. A family keepsake perhaps, a token of love, or a memento? We will never know.

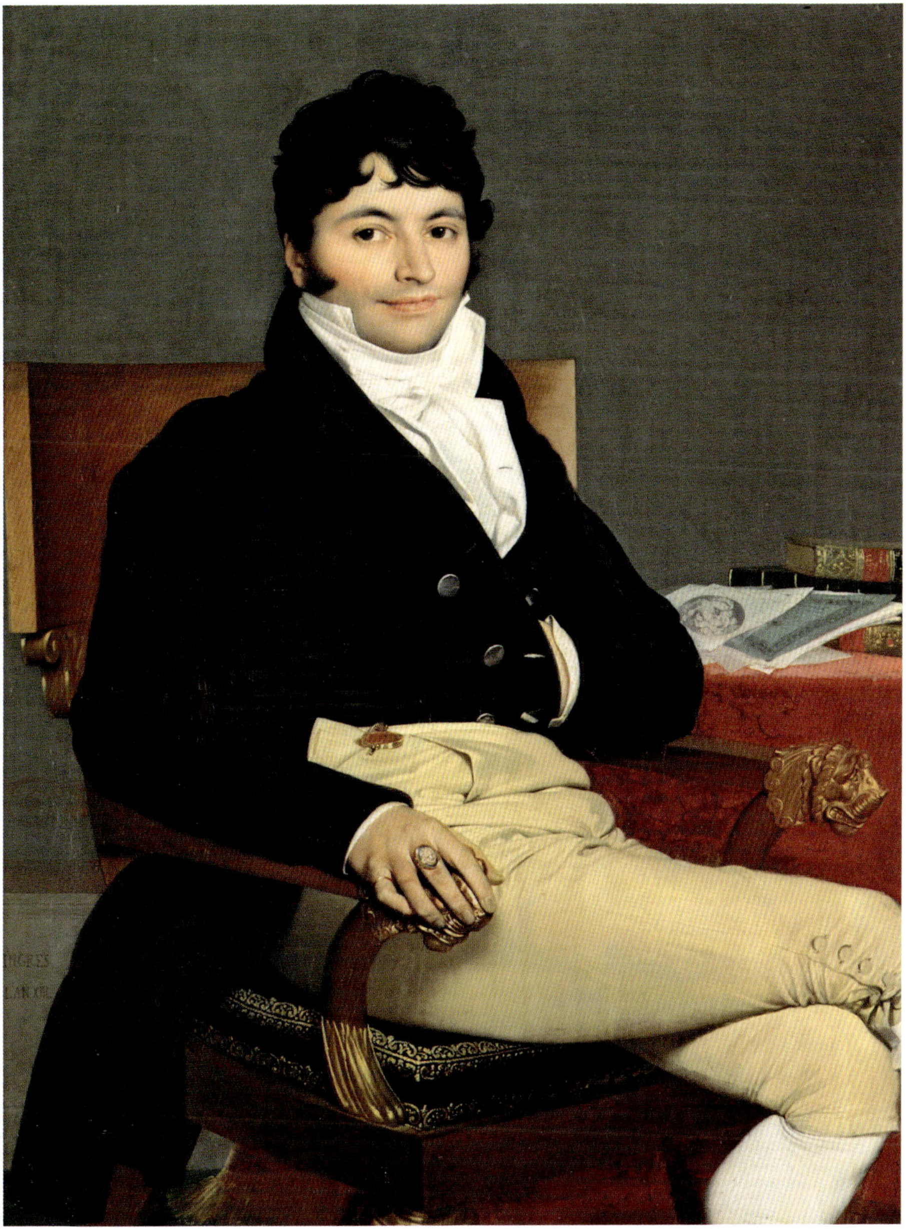

ÉVRARD BAPST (1771–1842)
FRÉDÉRIC BAPST (1789–1870)
Diadem of the Duchesse d'Angoulême, Paris, 1819–1820
Gold, silver, emeralds, and diamonds, 2 ½ × 7 ½ × 7 ½ in. (h. 6.8 cm, l. 19 cm, d. 17 cm)

This dazzling diadem comprises some one thousand and thirty-one diamonds and forty emeralds. The stones were taken from the crown treasury, an institution founded by Francis I in 1530, who, by letters patent, had established the crown jewels as an inalienable heirloom that each king was obliged to hand down to his successor, either intact or enlarged. And indeed both Louis XIV, and, after the Revolution (during which the treasury was ransacked), Napoleon I, did just that. The institution reflected a preoccupation with prestige as much as with financial concerns. For official ornaments, for example, monarchs were permitted to "borrow gemstones and cameos," with the proviso that they be restored to the treasury. It was a right taken up by many a sovereign.

During the Restoration of 1814–1830, the ornaments of Marie-Louise were partly altered and remounted for the Duchesse d'Angoulême by the house of Bapst, jewelers to the court since Louis XV. The duchess was the former Madame Royale (princess royal), eldest daughter of Louis XVI, who had been one of the captives in the Temple, and she exerted considerable sway over her uncle, Louis XVIII.

Two bracelets and a ruby diadem that belonged to her and are preserved in the Louvre issue from the same source. The emerald diadem was also worn by Empress Eugénie. In 1887, the French State did what no monarch had ever dared to do previously: it sold off the crown jewels. With rare exceptions, all the jewels were dispersed in a public sale attended by jewelers from around the world. The diadem was taken to England following its sale, but was purchased by the Amis du Louvre in 2002.

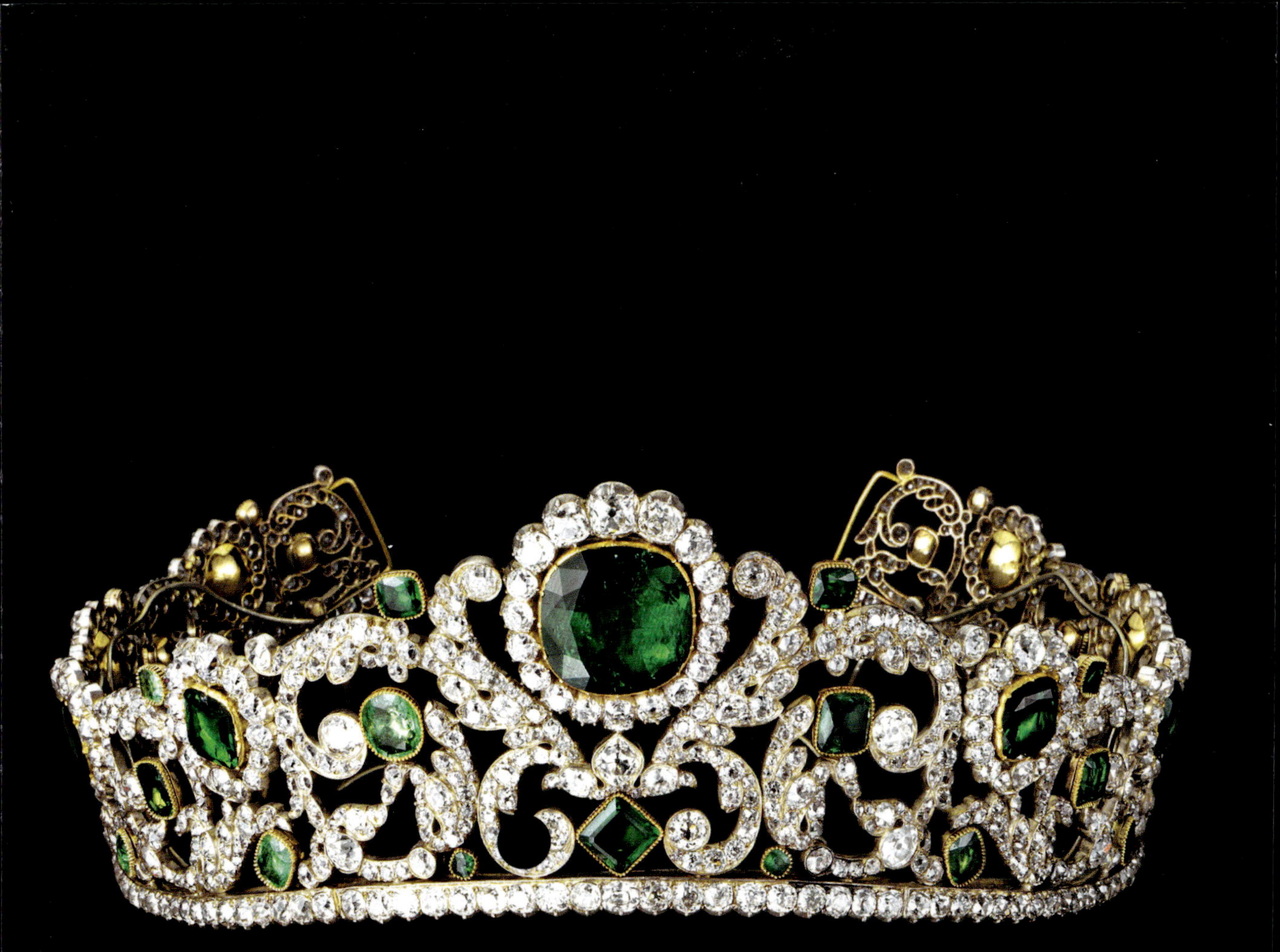

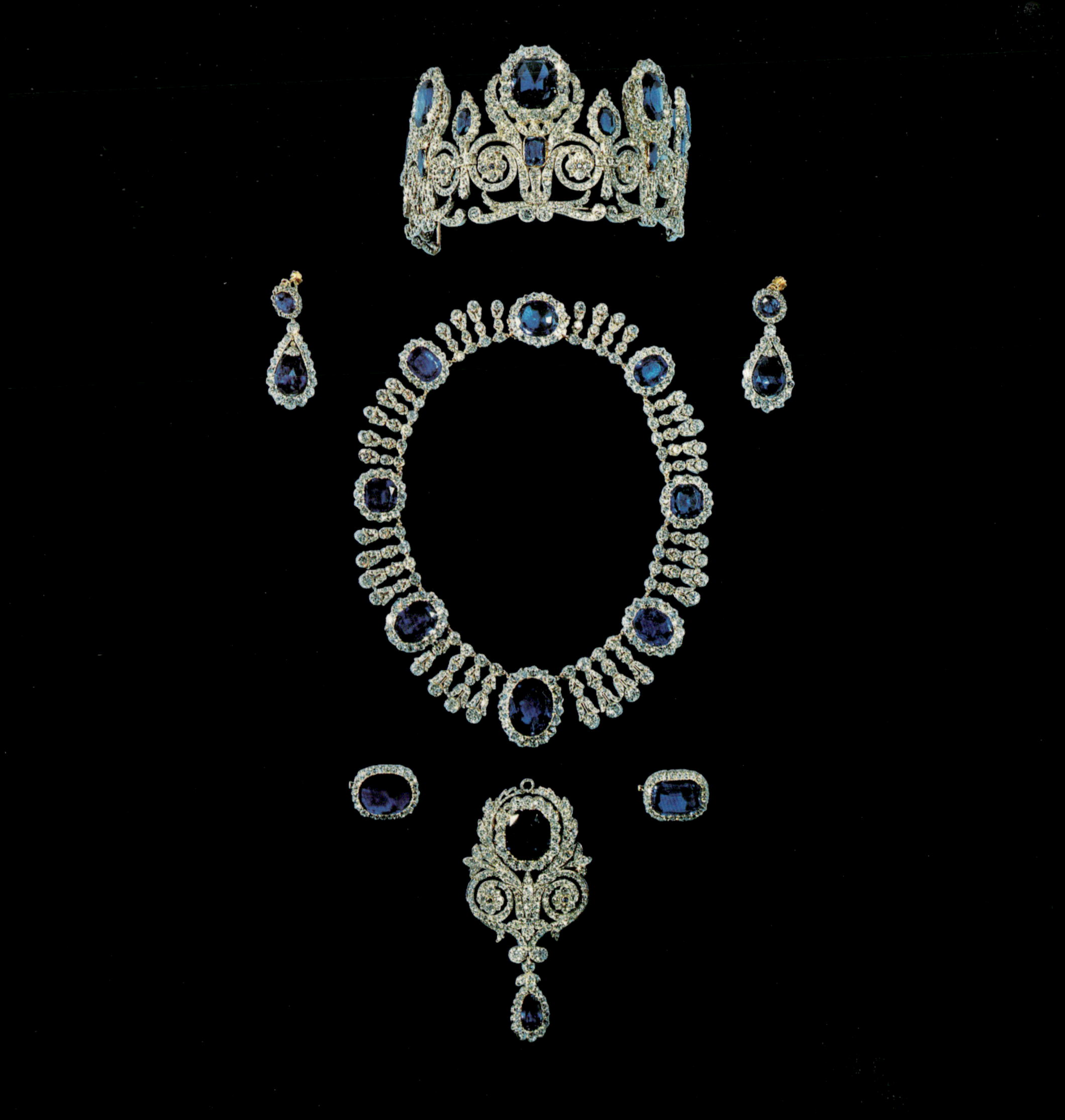

ANONYMOUS
Parure of Queen Marie-Amélie (1782–1866)
Diadem, necklace, earrings, and brooch
Paris, beginning and third quarter of the nineteenth century
Sapphires, diamonds, gold, and silver; diadem, h. 2 ¼ in., d. 4 ¼ in. (h. 6.20 cm, d. 10.70 cm)

Historic jewels that have been passed down to the present-day are often reminders of the private lives of the sovereigns who owned them. This remarkable parure, boasting more than three thousand diamonds and thirty-nine Ceylon sapphires, is a prime example, as it had more than one owner and was transformed several times over the years.

For the members of the exiled Bonaparte family who once reigned over Europe, the loss of their titles and wealth on the fall of the Empire demanded sacrifices, not the least of which were their innumerable jewels. In 1821, Queen Hortense (1783–1837), daughter of Empress Josephine, was forced to dispose of the sapphire parure that had formed part of her personal effects. It was purchased by Louis-Philippe, then Duc d'Orléans, as a present for his wife, Marie-Amélie, who is seen wearing it in a picture by Louis Hersent painted in 1826 and conserved at the Musée des Arts Décoratifs in Paris. In the painting the eye is immediately drawn to the splendid hat ornament, which was actually the parure's diadem: as taste and fashion evolve, so jewels, too, must change. The diadem was cut down and the sapphires reused in the brooch, which was reworked by Bapst. The two buttons for the gown are also a later addition.

After Marie-Amélie, the piece remained in the Orléans family, with Isabelle d'Orléans-Bragance (1911–2003) the last to have worn it. In 1985, her husband, the Comte de Paris, the last pretender to the throne of France (1908–1999), ceded it to the French State, thus ending an ownership that had lasted since 1821. It is now one of the most admired jewels in the Gallery of Apollo at the Louvre.

JEAN-VALENTIN MOREL (1794–1860)
HENRI DUPONCHEL (1794–1868)
Bracelet, Paris, c. 1845
Molten and engraved gold and fine pearls, h. 1 ⅛ in., l. 7 ¼ in., th. 1 ⅛ in.
(h. 2.8 cm, l. 18.2 cm, th. 2.8 cm)

Around 1840, the bracelet was the prize piece in any ensemble of jewelry, and women would wear more than one on each arm. Naturalism and sentimentalism often go hand in hand, as illustrated by this bracelet in the shape of an oak branch entwined in ivy. In the center, a nest on a stem contains three pearl eggs, with, on one side, a bird mounting guard and, on the other, a lizard on the lookout for a meal. The subject of a bird defending its nest against a reptile remained in vogue for twenty or so years, decorating brooches and tiepins. The bracelet's creators were Morel and Duponchel, both goldsmiths and jewelers, who, in the wake of Émile Froment-Meurice (1837–1913), had become master craftsmen of the Romantic period, producing the kind of "charming trinkets a woman's hand likes to caress": seals, bottle-cases, incense-burners, etc. Technological advances in metalwork made such "trinkets" possible. The lengthy and meticulous work of chasing and engraving metal had for the most part been ousted by casting and stamping, thereby increasing output and keeping costs down, without necessarily detracting from the inventiveness and redeployment of forms from the past that characterized the period. Since 1867 jewelers of all kinds had been awarded diplomas at World Fairs.

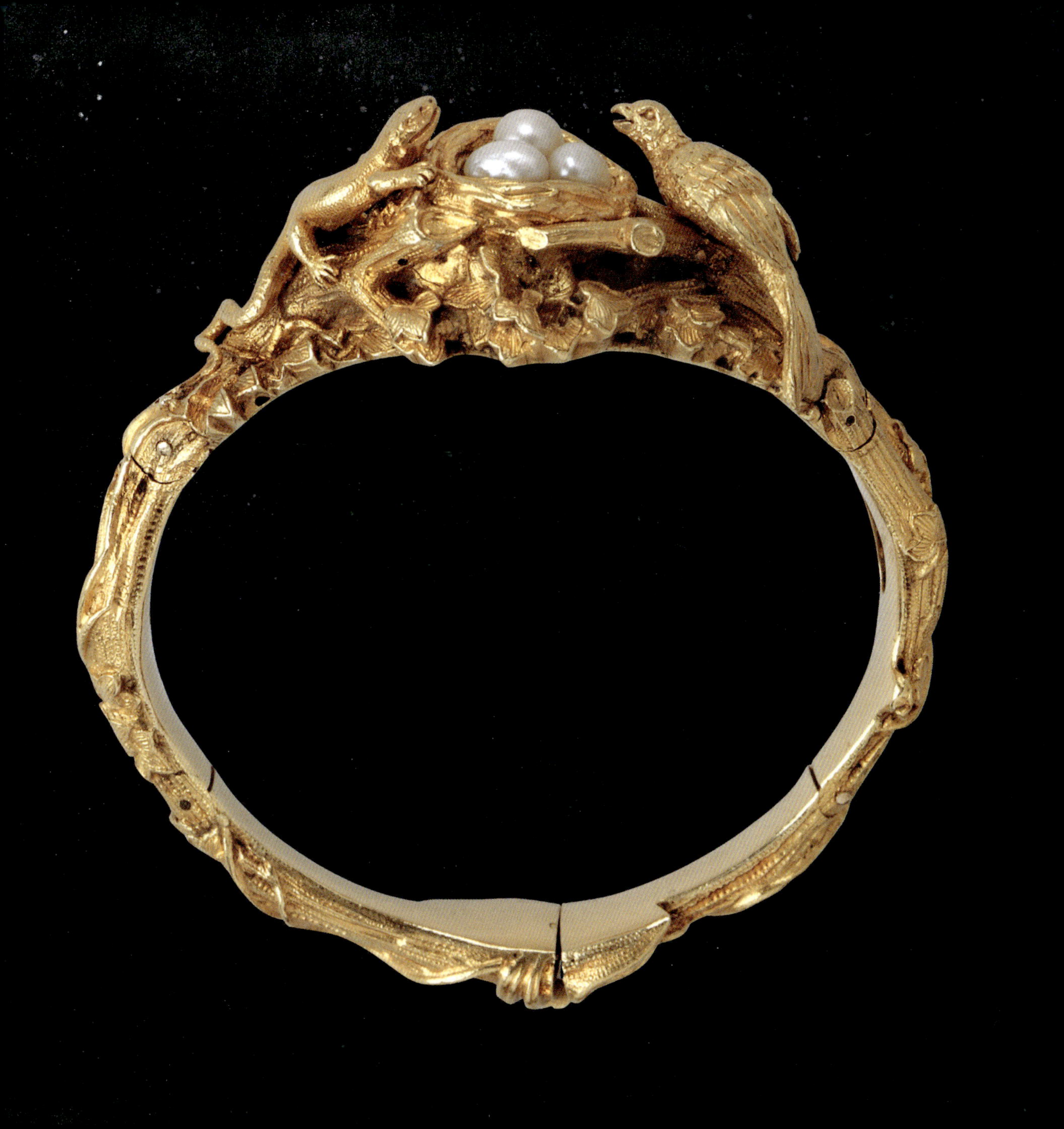

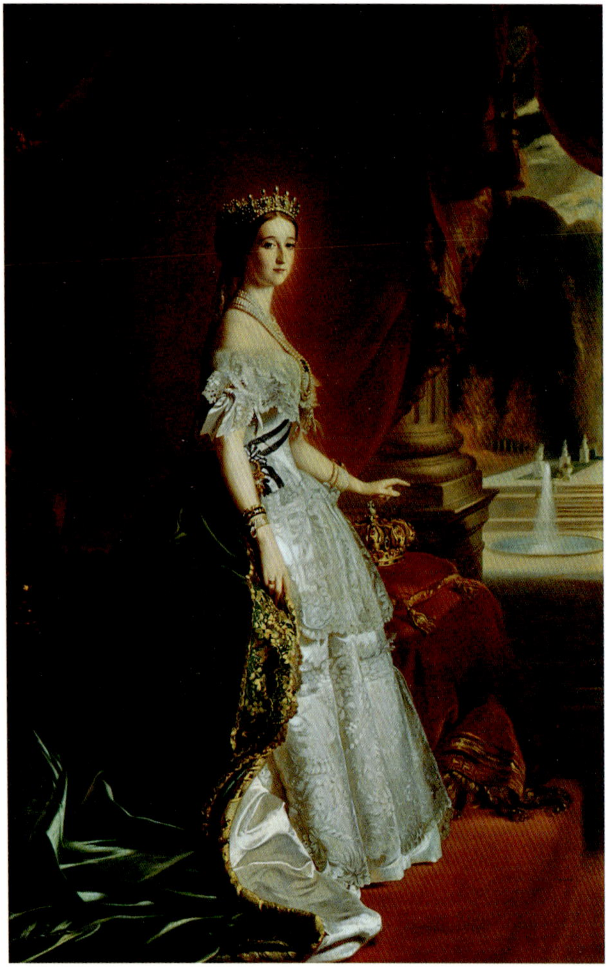

PIERRE-DÉSIRÉ GUILLEMET (1827–1863), ***AFTER FRANZ XAVER WINTERHALTER***
Portrait of Empress Eugénie, 1856–1857
Oil on canvas, 7 ft. 9 ¼ in. × 5 ft. 2 ¼ in. (2.42 × 1.58 m)

Commissioned by the French State in 1856, this portrait, like that of Napoleon III, is one of many copies of the painting of Empress Eugénie executed by Winterhalter following the proclamation of the Empire in 1852. These replicas were intended to hang in official buildings throughout France. Represented full-length, the empress appears as the delicate beauty who so bewitched Louis-Napoléon Bonaparte when he first met her when she was still Eugénia, Countess of Teba, the daughter of a Spanish grandee, the Count of Montijo. She sports a diadem and a coronet of pearls. With her hand, she gestures towards the crown with its gold rings lined with diamonds and engraved-gold eagles, a masterpiece by the jeweler Alexandre-Gabriel Lemonnier.

ALEXANDRE-GABRIEL LEMONNIER (1808–1884)
Diadem of Empress Eugénie, Paris, 1853
Pearls, diamonds, and silver, h. 2 ¾ in.,
l. 7 ½ in., d. 7 ¼ in. (h. 7 cm, l. 19 cm, d. 18.5 cm)

Seemingly torn between modesty and a passion for display, Empress Eugénie took great care with her appearance. Hugely admired for her beauty and elegance, she was given a vast number of jewels as personal presents by Napoleon III. The empress also made ample use of the crown jewels, modifying them as she saw fit. Some of the finest diamonds from the French royal treasury—for example, the Hortensia, acquired by Louis XIV, the Regent, worn by Louis XV and Napoleon I, and the Mazarins, having once belonged to Christina of Sweden—passed through her hands. Out of these, she had objects made such as tasseled brooches, as well as shoulder knots and bows, bodice fronts, or nets and stars for the hair. As fond of gems as the emperor's cousin, Princess Mathilde, Eugénie possessed some splendid necklaces and *rivières* (single strands of precious stones), with several rows of pearls of unequal lengths in what was a new departure for the time. The craftsman ordered by Napoleon III to create this diadem, Gabriel Lemonnier, employed gems from the crown jewels: two-hundred-and-twelve round and pear-shaped pearls from the Orient set in foliate scrollwork containing almost two thousand diamonds.

This exceptional piece was sold in 1887 to a German prince, during the sale of the crown jewels by the French State. Albert von Thurn und Taxis acquired this and one of the empress's corsage ornaments for his wife Marguerite as a wedding present. Worn regularly by the princesses of this exceptionally wealthy family for more than a century, the diadem was finally sold at auction in 1992 and acquired by the Société des Amis du Louvre, thus returning to France.

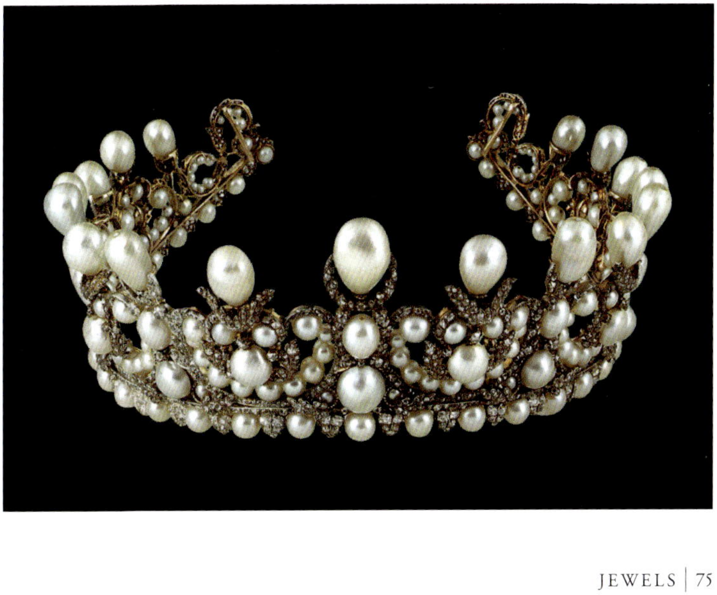

LIST OF ILLUSTRATIONS

P. 21
After **François Clouet**
Portrait of Elizabeth of Austria (1554–1592), sixteenth century
Oil on wood, 14 × 10 ¼ in. (36 × 26 cm)
Inv. 3254
Department of Paintings

P. 22
Attributed to **François Quesnel** (1543–1616)
Henry III King of France, c. 1582–1586
Oil on wood, 26 × 20 ½ in. (66 × 52 cm)
Inv. R.F. 3964
Department of Paintings

P. 23
After **Andrea Solario** (c. 1465–1524)
Portrait of Charles d'Amboise, c. 1507
Oil on wood, 29 ½ × 20 ½ in. (75 × 52 cm)
Inv. 674
Department of Paintings

P. 24–25
Anonymous
Pendant in the shape of a ship
Italy (?), second half of the sixteenth century
Enameled gold, pearls, and paint under crystal, 4 × 2 ⅜ in. (10.3 × 5.9 cm)
Inv. MRR 221
Department of Decorative Arts

P. 26
Leonardo da Vinci (1452–1519)
Portrait of a Lady (La Belle Ferronnière), 1592
Oil on wood, 24 ¾ × 17 ¾ in. (63 × 45 cm)
Inv. 778
Department of Paintings

P. 27
Jean-Baptiste Camille Corot (1796–1875)
Woman with a Pearl (*La Femme à la perle*), c. 1868
Oil on canvas 30 in × 17 ½ in. (70 × 55 cm)
Inv. R.F. 2040
Department of Paintings

P. 28–29
Paolo Caliari, *called* Veronese (1528–1588)
Venetian Lady known as *La Bella Nani*, c. 1560
Oil on canvas 3 ft. 10 ¾ in. × 3 ft. 4 ½ in. (1.19 × 1.03 m)
Inv. R.F. 2111
Department of Paintings

P. 30–31
Paolo Caliari, *called* Veronese (1528–1588)
The Wedding at Cana, 1562–1564
Oil on canvas, 12 ft. 2 ½ in. × 32 ft. 7 ⅜ in. (6.77 × 9.94 m)
Inv. 142
Department of Paintings

P. 32
Anonymous
Ring
Italy, sixteenth century
Gold enamel and emerald, d. 1 ¼ in. (3.2 cm)
Inv. OA 5631
Department of Decorative Arts

P. 33
Hans Holbein, *called* the Younger (1497–1543)
Portrait of Anne of Cleves (1515–1557), 1539
Oil on parchment, 25 ½ × 18 in. (65 × 46 cm)
Inv. 1348
Department of Paintings

P. 34
Giovanni da Modena (active c. 1398–1456)
Virgin and Child, beginning of the fifteenth century
Oil on wood, 25 ¼ × 17 ¾ in. (64 × 45 cm)
Inv. R.F. 1983-45
Department of Paintings

P. 35
Anonymous
Pectoral cross
Spain or Italy, second third of the sixteenth century
Enameled gold, rock crystal, and pearls, 2 ⅞ × 1 ¾ in. (7.4 × 4.5 cm)
Inv. OA 6177
Department of Decorative Arts

P. 36
Lucas Cranach the Elder (1472–1553)
Portrait of John Frederick, the Magnanimous, Elector of Saxony, 1531
Oil on wood, 25 ¼ × 16 ½ in. (64 × 42 cm)
Inv. 1184
Department of Paintings

P. 37
Abu'l Hasan Nadir ar-Zaman *and* Hashim
Djahangir Holding a Portrait of his Father, Emperor Akbar, India, c. 1605
Miniature on paper with gouache and gold, 7 ¼ × 4 ½ in. (18.3 × 11.6 cm)
Inv. 3676b
Collection of Drawings and Miniatures, on deposit at the Musée Guimet, Musée National des Arts Asiatiques, Paris

P. 38–39
Quentin Metsys (1466–1530)
The Moneylender and his Wife, 1514
Oil on wood, 28 × 26 ¾ in. (71 × 68 cm)
Inv. 1444
Department of Paintings

P. 40
French school
Double portrait
Early seventeenth century
Oil on wood, 28 ¾ × 37 ¾ in. (73 × 96 cm)
Inv. R.F. 1967 9
Department of Paintings

P. 41
Claude Champagneux *or* **Champagnieu**, watchmaker
Octagonal watch
Lyon, second quarter of the seventeenth century
Rock crystal, brass, 2 × 1 ¼ × ⅞ in. (5.2 × 3.1 × 2.3 cm)
Inv. OA 10060
Department of Decorative Arts

P. 42
François de Hecq, watchmaker
Carriage watch with the coat-of-arms of Cardinal Richelieu
Orleans, c. 1640
Silver, gilt brass, d. 4 ⅛ in., th. 12 ¼ in. (d. 10.4 cm, th. 4.8 cm)
Inv. OA 12115
Department of Decorative Arts

P. 43
The Polish Eagle of Louis XIV
Paris, mid-seventeenth century
Gold, enamel, pearls, emeralds, rubies, and garnets, 4 ⅜ in. (11.10 cm)
Inv. MR 418
Department of Decorative Arts

P. 44
Hyacinthe Rigaud (1659–1743)
Louis XIV (1638–1715), 1701
Oil on canvas, 9 ft. 1 in. × 6 ft. 4 ½ in. (2.77 × 1.94 m)
Inv. 7492
Department of Paintings

P. 45
Diamond known as the "Regent"
1698
140.64 carats
Inv. MV 1017
Department of Decorative Arts

P. 46
Anonymous
Star of the Order of the Holy Spirit
Paris, mid-eighteenth century
Gold, silver, diamonds, and ruby, d. 4 ⅜ in. (11 cm)
Inv. OA 9527
Department of Decorative Arts

P. 47
Maurice-Quentin De La Tour (1704–1788)
Louis-Stanislas-Xavier of France, Comte de Provence, eighteenth century
Pastel on paper, 19 ½ × 17 ¾ in. (50 × 45 cm)
Inv. 27617
Department of Paintings

P. 49
Charles-Simon Boucher, chatelaine, Paris, 1751–1752
Jacques-Jérôme Gudin, watch, Paris, 1750–1751
Round watch with matching chatelaine
Gold, gilt brass, enamel, diamond, and agate, d. 1 ¾ in., th. 1 in. (d. 4. 80 cm, th. 2.60 cm)
Inv. OA 8394
Department of Decorative Arts

P. 50–51
Anton-Raphael Mengs (1728–1779)
Maria-Luisa of Parma, Princess of the Asturias, 1765
Oil on canvas, 4 ft. 2 ¾ in. × 3 ft. 2 in (129 × 97 cm)
Inv. 1455
Department of Paintings

P. 52–53
Antoine-Jean Gros (1771–1835)
Madame Pasteur, 1795–1796
Oil on canvas, 34 ¼ × 26 ⅜ in. (87 × 67 cm)
Inv. R.F. 1948-42
Department of Paintings

P. 54
Jacques-Louis David (1748–1825)
The Coronation of the Emperor and Empress (the Consecration), 1805–1807
Oil on canvas, 20 ft. 7 ½ in. × 32 ft. 1 in. (6.29 × 9.79 m)
Inv. 3699
Department of Paintings

P. 55
Pierre-Louis Bouvier (1765–1836)
Portrait of Empress Josephine, 1812
Miniature on ivory, d. 3 ⅝ in. (9.3 cm)
Inv. R.F. 30670
Department of Paintings

P. 56–57
Marie-Guillemine Benoist (1768–1826)
Portrait of a Black Woman, Salon of 1800
Oil on canvas, 31 ⅞ × 25 ½ in. (81 × 65 cm)
Inv. 2508
Department of Paintings

P. 59
François-Regnault Nitot (1779–1853)
Parure of the Empress Marie-Louise, Paris, 1810
Gold and glass micro-mosaic, necklace: 17 ¾ in. (45 cm); bracelets: 7 ¼ in. (18.5 cm); comb: 4 ⅜ in. (11 cm); earrings: 1 ¾ in. (4.3 cm)
Inv. OA 11963
Department of Decorative Arts

P. 60
Théodore Chassériau (1819–1856)
The Toilet of Esther or *Esther Preparing herself to Meet King Assuerus*, 1841
Oil on canvas, 18 × 14 in. (45.5 × 35.5 cm)
Inv. R.F. 3900
Department of Paintings

P. 61
Anonymous
Necklace, Cerveteri, 480–460 BCE
Gold, filigree, and stamping, 1 ¼ × 8 ½ in. (3.3 × 21.4 cm)
Inv. Bj 514
Department of Greek, Etruscan, and Roman Antiquities

P. 62–63
French School
The Three Ladies of Ghent, 1816–1817
Oil on canvas, 4 ft. 4 in. × 3 ft. 5 in. (1.32 × 1.05 m)
Inv. R.F. 902
Department of Paintings

P. 64–65
Jean-Auguste-Dominique Ingres (1780–1867)
Madame Marcotte, 1826
Oil on canvas, 36 ½ × 29 in. (93 × 74 cm)
Inv. R.F. 2398
Department of Paintings

P. 66–67
Jean-Auguste-Dominique Ingres (1780–1867)
Monsieur Rivière, 1804
Oil on canvas, 3 ft. 9 ¼ in. × 35 ½ in. (115 × 90 cm)
Inv. M.I. 1445
Department of Paintings

P. 69
Évrard Bapst (1771–1842)
Frédéric Bapst (1789–1870)
Diadem of the Duchesse d'Angoulême, Paris, 1819–1820
Gold, silver, emeralds, and diamonds, 2 ½ × 7 ½ × 7 ½ in. (h. 6.8 cm, l. 19 cm, d. 17 cm)
Inv. OA 11982
Department of Decorative Arts

P. 70
Parure of Queen Marie-Amélie (1782–1866), diadem, necklace, earrings, brooch
Paris, beginning and third quarter of the nineteenth century
Sapphires, diamonds, gold, and silver; diadem, h. 2 ¼ in., d. 4 ¼ in. (h. 6.20 cm, d. 10.70 cm)
Inv. OA 11030 to 11036
Department of Decorative Arts

P. 73
Jean-Valentin Morel (1794–1860)
Henri Duponchel (1794–1868)
Bracelet, Paris, c. 1845
Molten and engraved gold and fine pearls, h. 1 ⅛ in., l. 7 ¼ in., th. 1 ⅛ in. (h. 2.8 cm, l. 18.2 cm, th. 2.8 cm)
Inv. OA 11225
Department of Decorative Arts

P. 74
Pierre-Désiré Guillemet (1827–1863), ***after* Franz Xaver Winterhalter**
Portrait of Empress Eugénie, 1856–1857
Oil on canvas, 7 ft. 9 ¼ in. × 5 ft. 2 ¼ in. (2.42 × 1.58 m)
Inv. R.F. 20067
Department of Paintings

P. 75
Alexandre-Gabriel Lemonnier (1808–1884)
Diadem of Empress Eugénie, Paris, 1853
Pearls, diamonds, and silver, h. 2 ¾ in., l. 7 ½ in., d. 7 ¼ in. (h. 7 cm, l. 19 cm, d. 18.5 cm)
Inv. OA 11369
Department of Decorative Arts

PHOTOGRAPHIC CREDITS

© Erich Lessing: pages 18, 21, 22, 23, 27, 28–29, 30, 33, 34, 36, 38–9, 44, 45, 50–51, 52 56–57, 59, 60, 65, 66–67, 74

© RMN/All rights reserved: pages 20, 31, 46, 55, 70, 73, 75
© RMN/Franck Raux: page 26
© RMN/Jean-Gilles Berizzi: pages 13, 24–25, 32, 35, 41, 42, 69
© RMN/Les Frères Chuzeville: page 10
© RMN/Hervé Lewandowski: pages 12, 17
© RMN/Daniel Arnaudet: pages 16, 19, 43, 62–63
© RMN/Thierry Olivier: page 37
© RMN/Christian Jean/Jean Schormans: page 40
© RMN/Gérard Blot: page 47
© RMN/Varge: page 49
© RMN/Christian Jean: page 53
© RMN/Gérard Blot/Christian Jean: pages 61, 64

© 2007 Musée du Louvre/Angèle Dequier: page 4
© 2005 Musée du Louvre/Christian Décamps: page 11
© 2003 Musée du Louvre/Erich Lessing: cover
© 2003 Musée du Louvre/Erich Lessing: page 54
© 2005 Musée du Louvre/Erich Lessing: page 14
© Musée du Louvre/Georges Poncet: page 15

IN THE SAME SERIES

Cats in the Louvre
Dogs in the Louvre
Love in the Louvre